In Art: Knights

{Enjoying Great Art series}

Brought to you by

Bonnie Hardison

Books in the "Enjoying Great Art" Series by Catherine Jaime:
- *In Art: Animals*
- *In Art: Books*
- *In Art: Bridges*
- *In Art: Cats*
- *In Art: Christmas*
- *In Art: Eagles*
- *In Art: Food*
- *In Art: Hats*
- *In Art: Horses*
- *In Art: Leonardo*
- *In Art: Lighthouses*
- *In Art: New York City*
- *In Art: Parasols and Umbrellas*
- *In Art: Self-Portraits*
- *In Art: Trees*
- *In Art: Turkey*

Books in the series by Deirdre Fuller:
- *In Art: America's National Parks*
- *In Art: Art*
- *In Art: Butterflies*
- *In Art: Chickens*
- *In Art: Clowns*
- *In Art: Dogs*
- *In Art: Farms*
- *In Art: Pugs*
- *In Art: U.S. Presidents*

Paintings are in the public domain or used with permission from the artists.

Knights are frequently thought of in fairy tales or legends. Often, we think of them doing great, impressive, and heroic deeds. But, do we think of them, when we think of great art?

This is a picture book, for all ages, of knights in art. The knight is presented differently in each picture. Please notice the differences and similarities in the pictures. These images span centuries. Notice the size, materials used to create the artwork, country, and current location of the art work. Some of the art work has more information available than others. Look at the colors, patterns, and textures in the pictures. Notice the backgrounds, presence of women, animals, and landscapes in the art work.

You can find more information about knights, by researching the following: Knighthood, Lords, the Middle Ages in Europe, Feudalism, Fiefdoms, and Chivalry

Most importantly, enjoy this book of Knights in art.

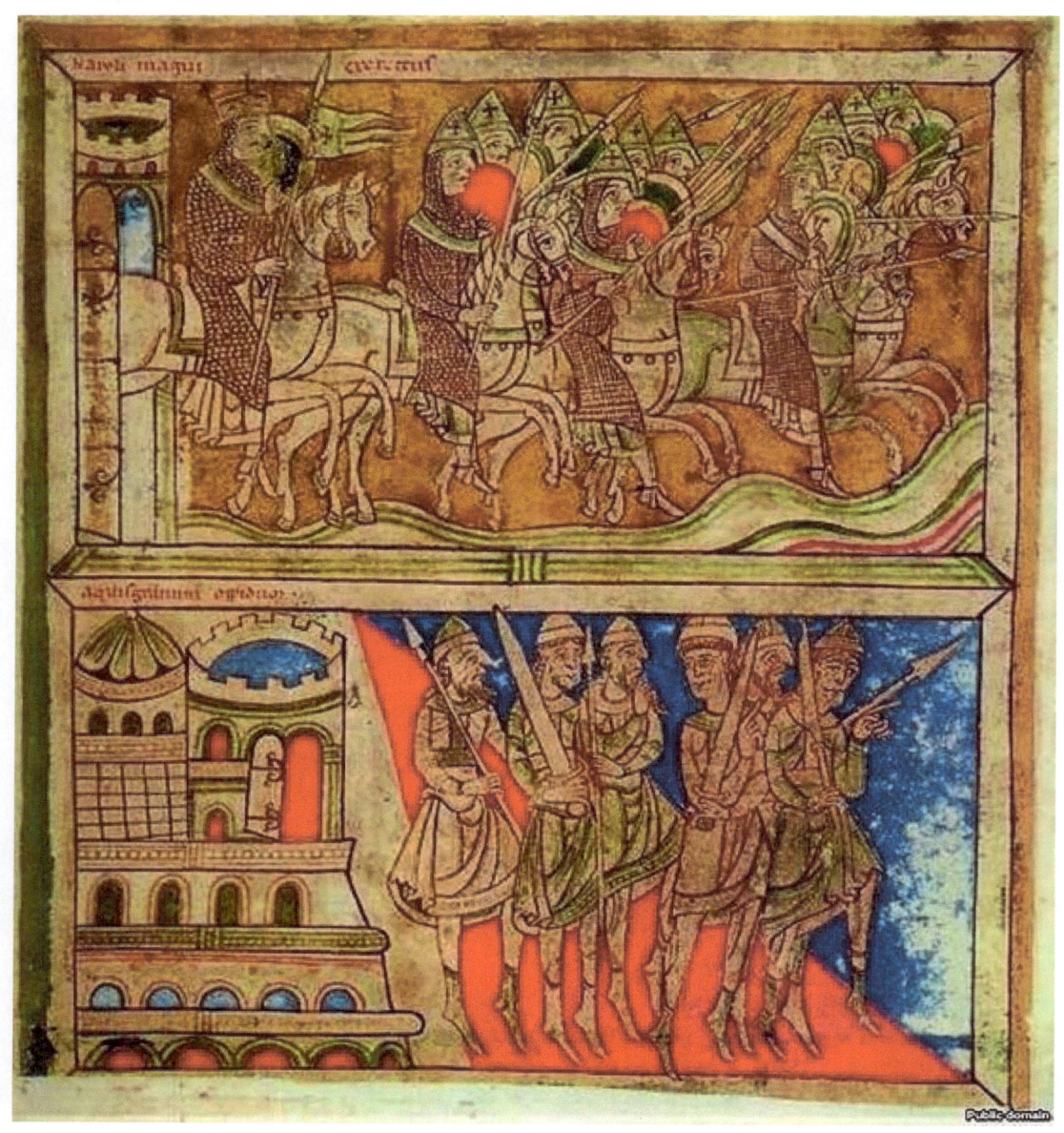

Charlemagne, Roland and the Knights on their way to Compostela, Spain

Unknown Artist

1135-1139AD

Codex Calixtinus (Liber Sancti Jacobi)

Folio 162v

Held in the Cathedral of Santiago de Compostela, Galicia (Spain)

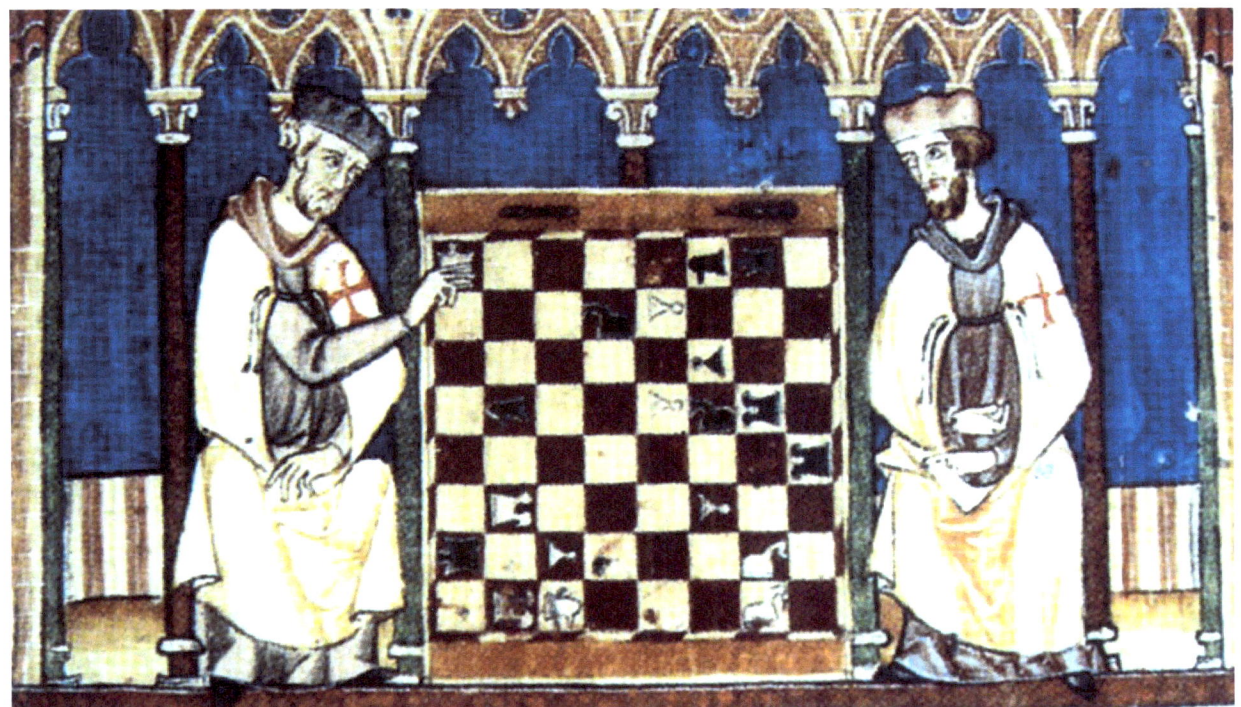

Knights Templar Playing Chess

Alphonse le Sage (also known as Alfonso X)

1283

Book Illustration

Biblioteca del Monasterio de El Escorial, ms T. I 6, fol. 25. Patrimonio Nacional, Spain

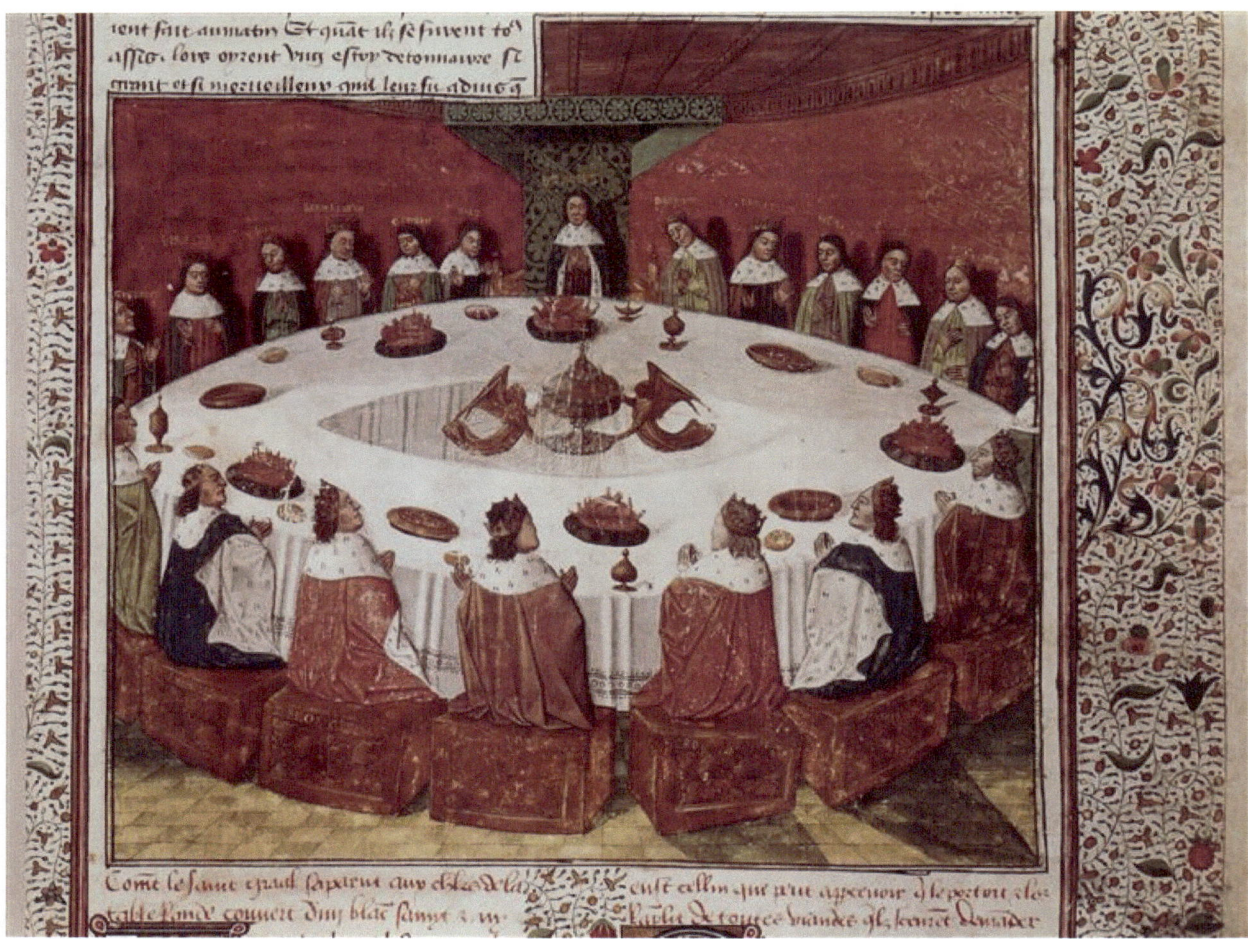

King Arthur and the Knights of the Round Table

Unknown artist

13th century

Painting on Paper

National Library of France, Paris

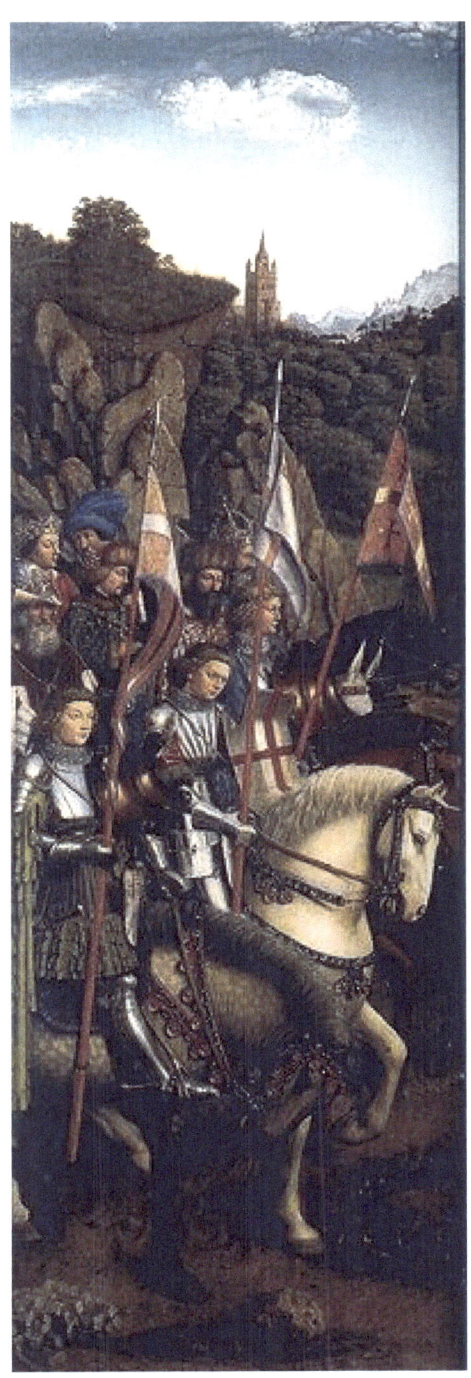

Knights of Christ (detail from the Ghent Altarpiece)

Jan Van Eyck

Completed 1432

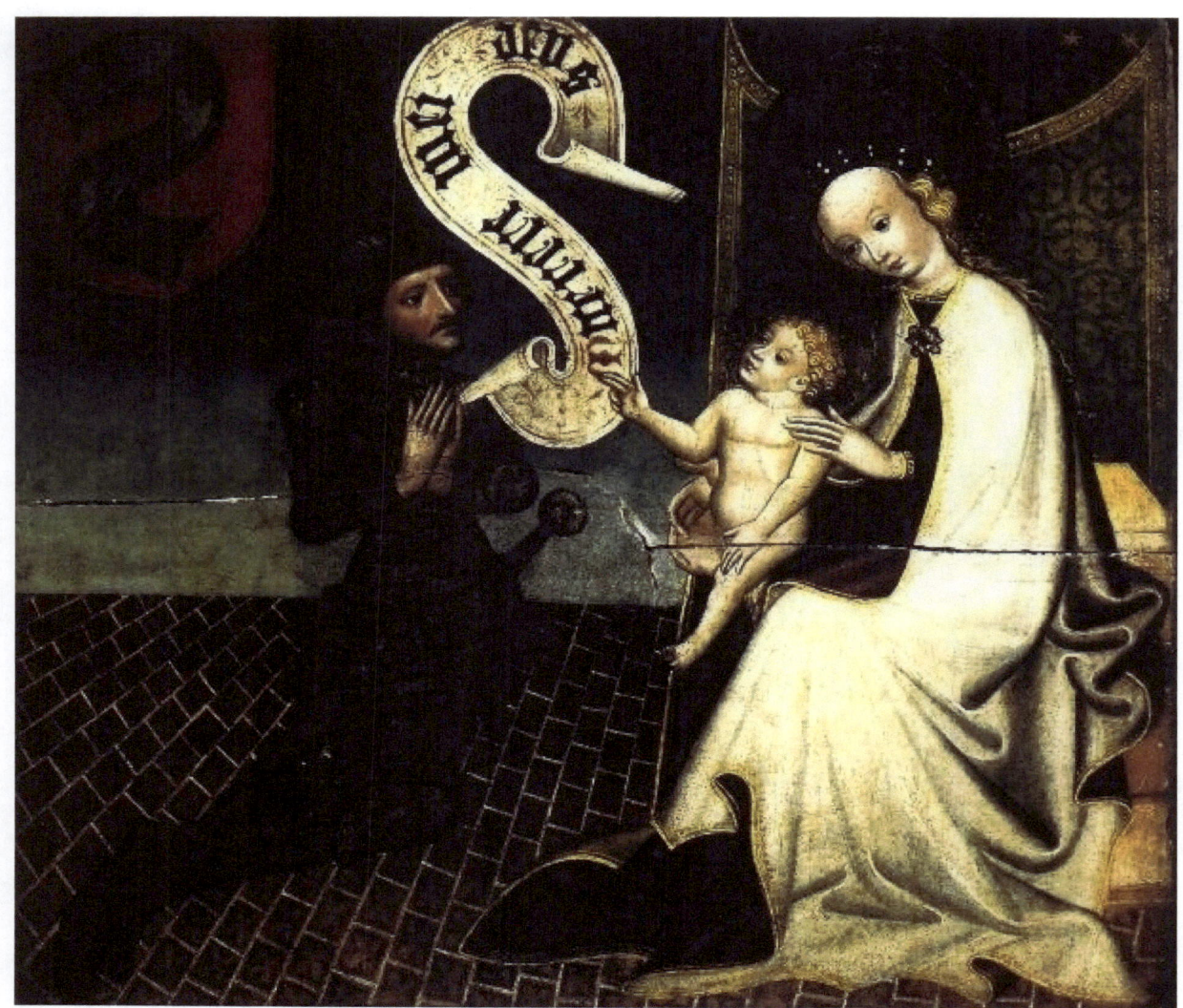

Epitaph of Jan of Ujazd

Unknown Artist, painted in Lesser Poland

Circa 1450

Tempera Paint on Panel

15.7in x 17.7in

Kept in the Wawel Royal Castle

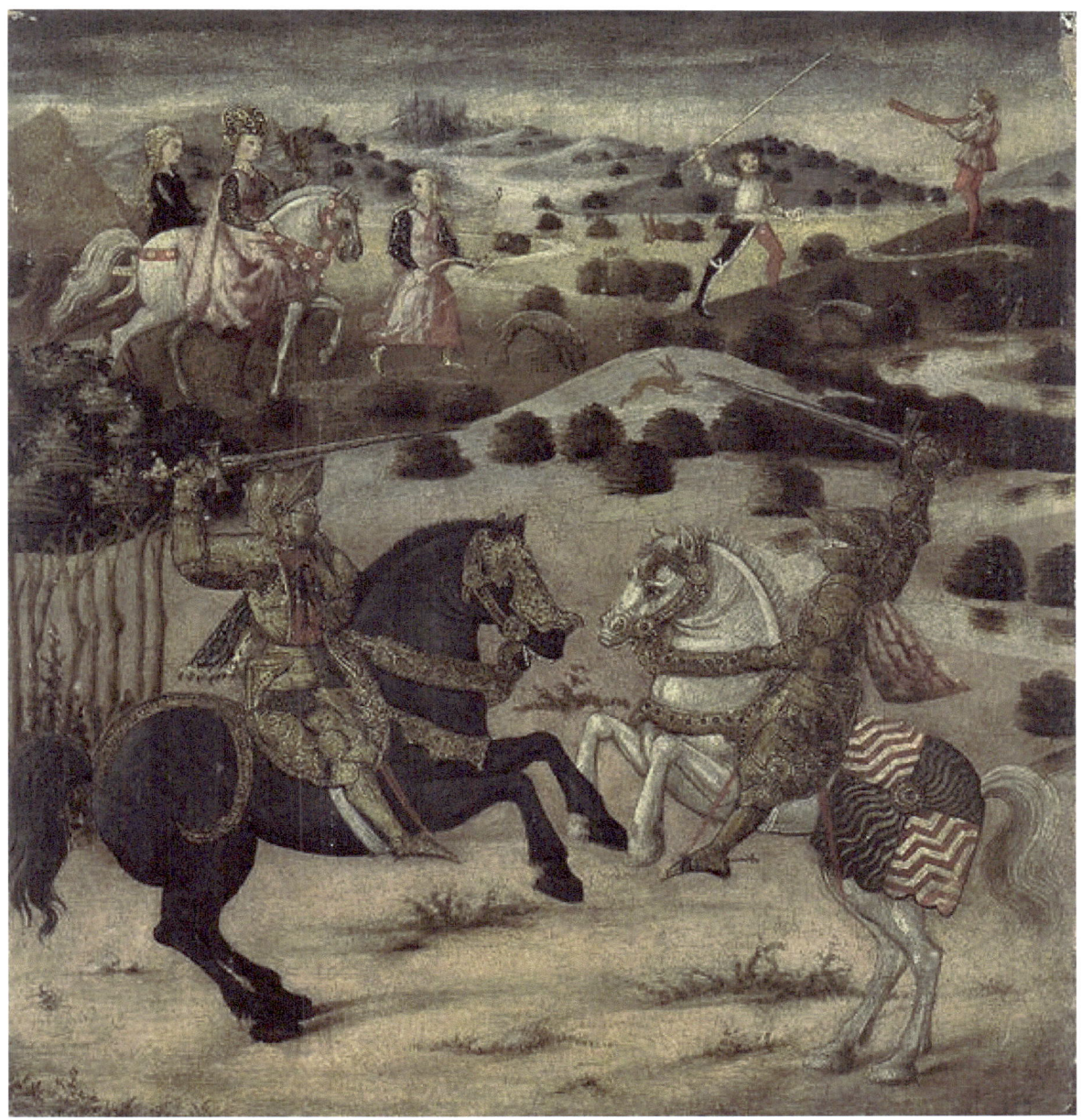

Tafereel uit een ridderlegende

Unknown Artist

Dated 1450-1474

Tempera on Panel

From Florence, Italy

15.7in x 16.5in

Rijksmuseum Amsterdam

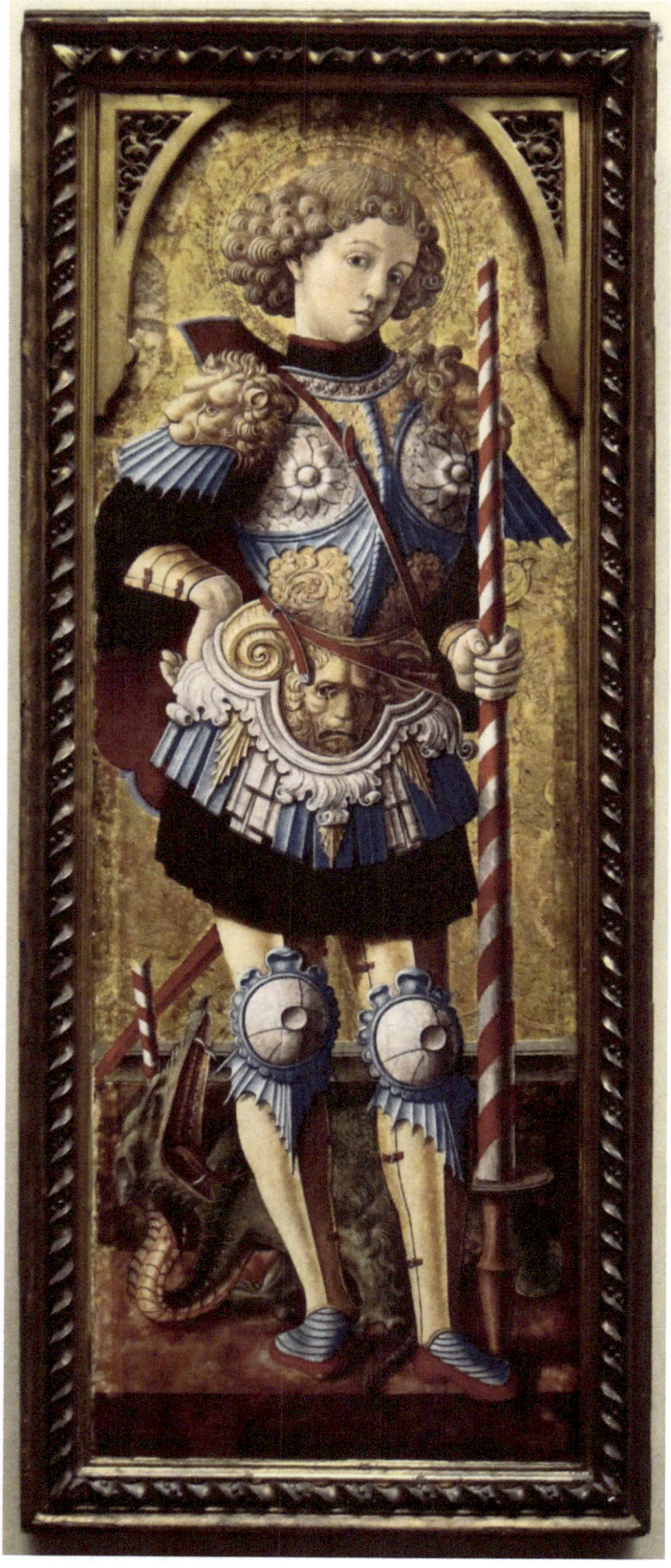

Saint George

Carlo Crivelli

Painted in 1472

Tempera on Wood

Metropolitan Museum of Art

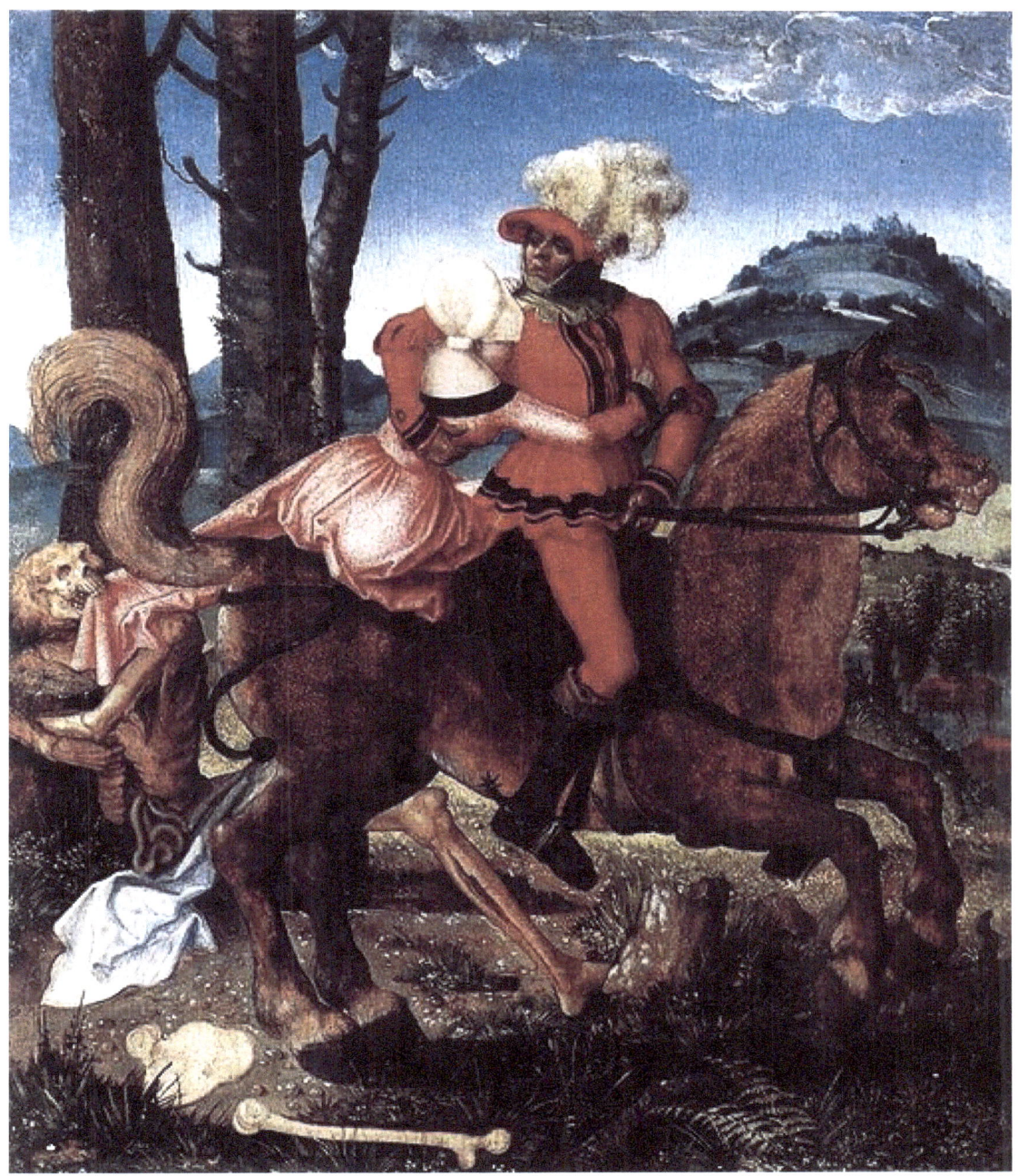

The Knight, The Young Girl, and Death

Hans Baldung

1505

Oil on Panel

139.8in x 116.5in

Louvre Museum, Paris

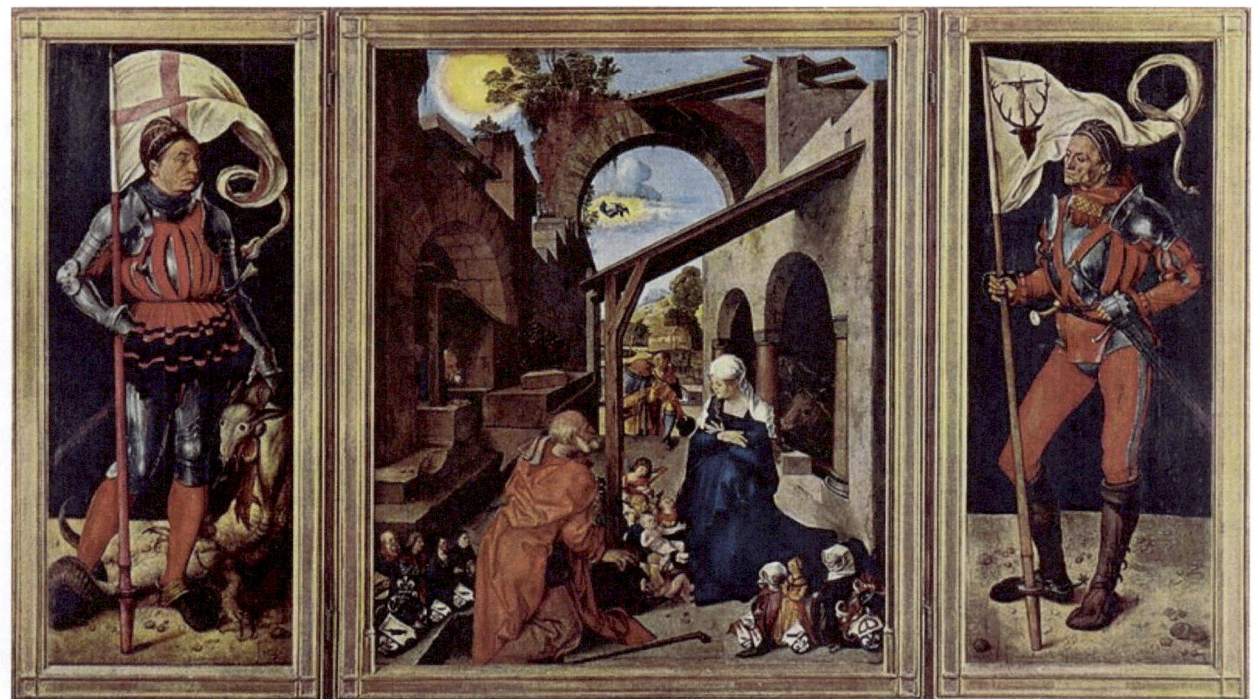

Paumgartner Altar

Albrect Dürer

After 1503

Color on Wood

61.8in x 24in (left wing)

61.1in x 49.7in(center portion)

61.8in x 24in (right wing)

Alte Pinakothek

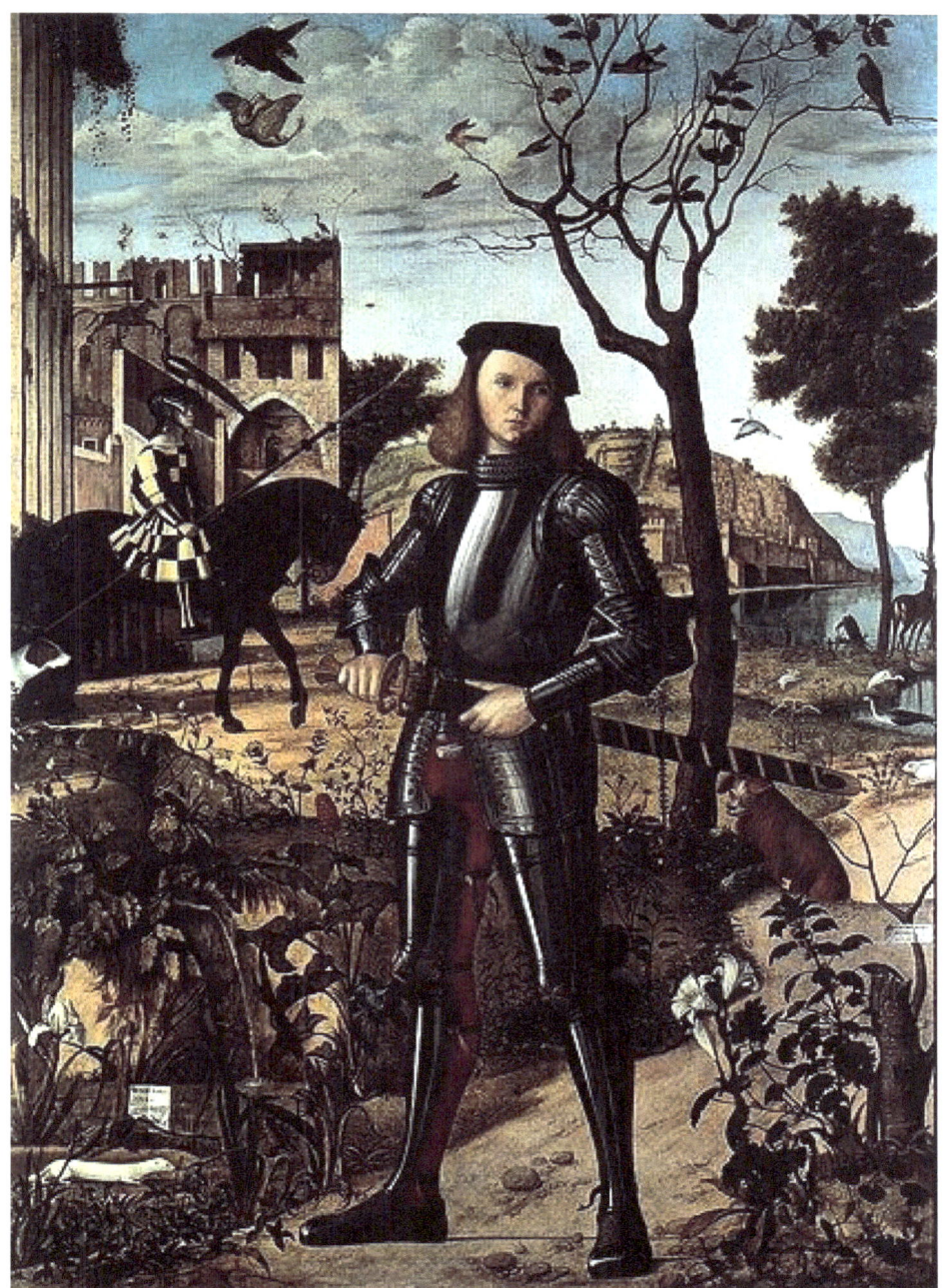

Young Knight in a Landscape

Vittore Carpaccio

Painted in the year 1510

Oil on Canvas

59.6in x 86in

Venice, Italy

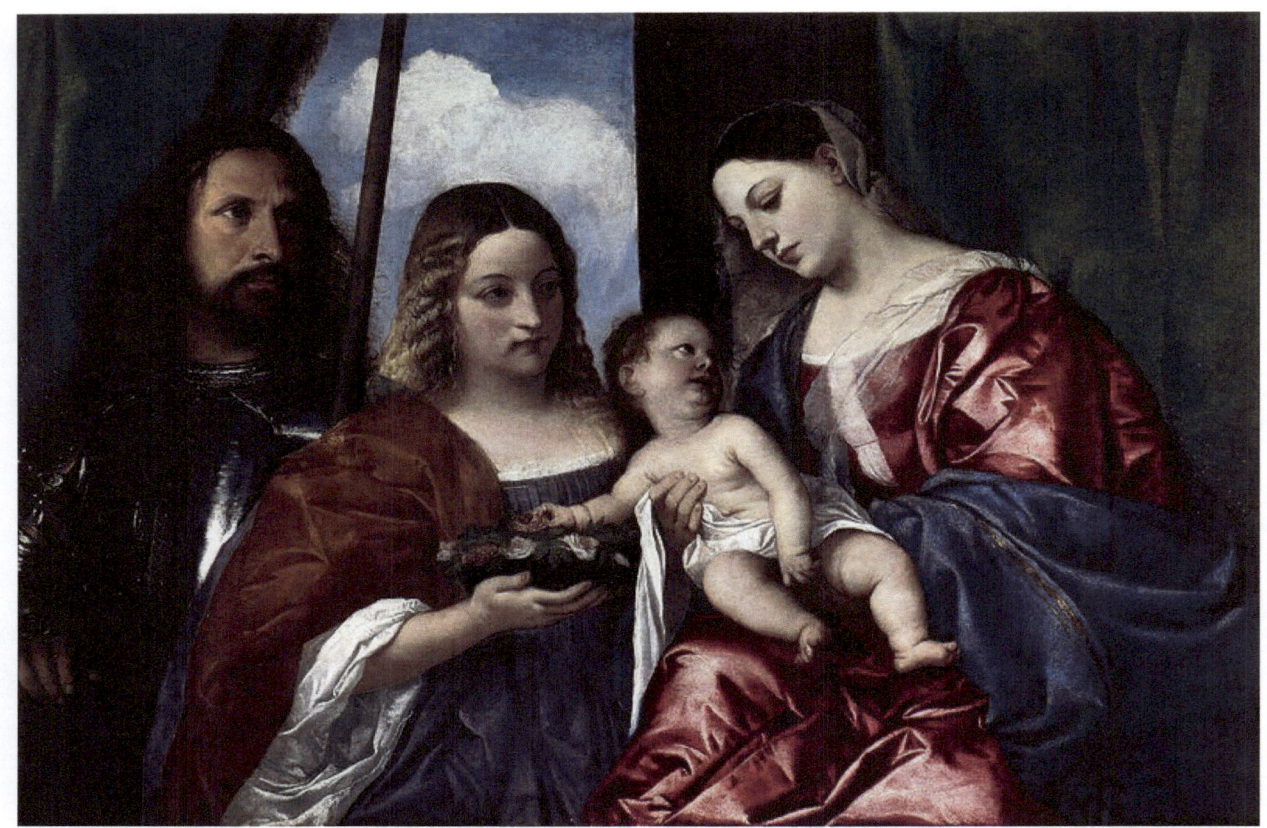

Madonna and Child with Saint Dorothy and Saint George

Titian

Between 1516 and 1520

Oil on Panel

33.9in x 51.2in

Prado Museum, Madrid

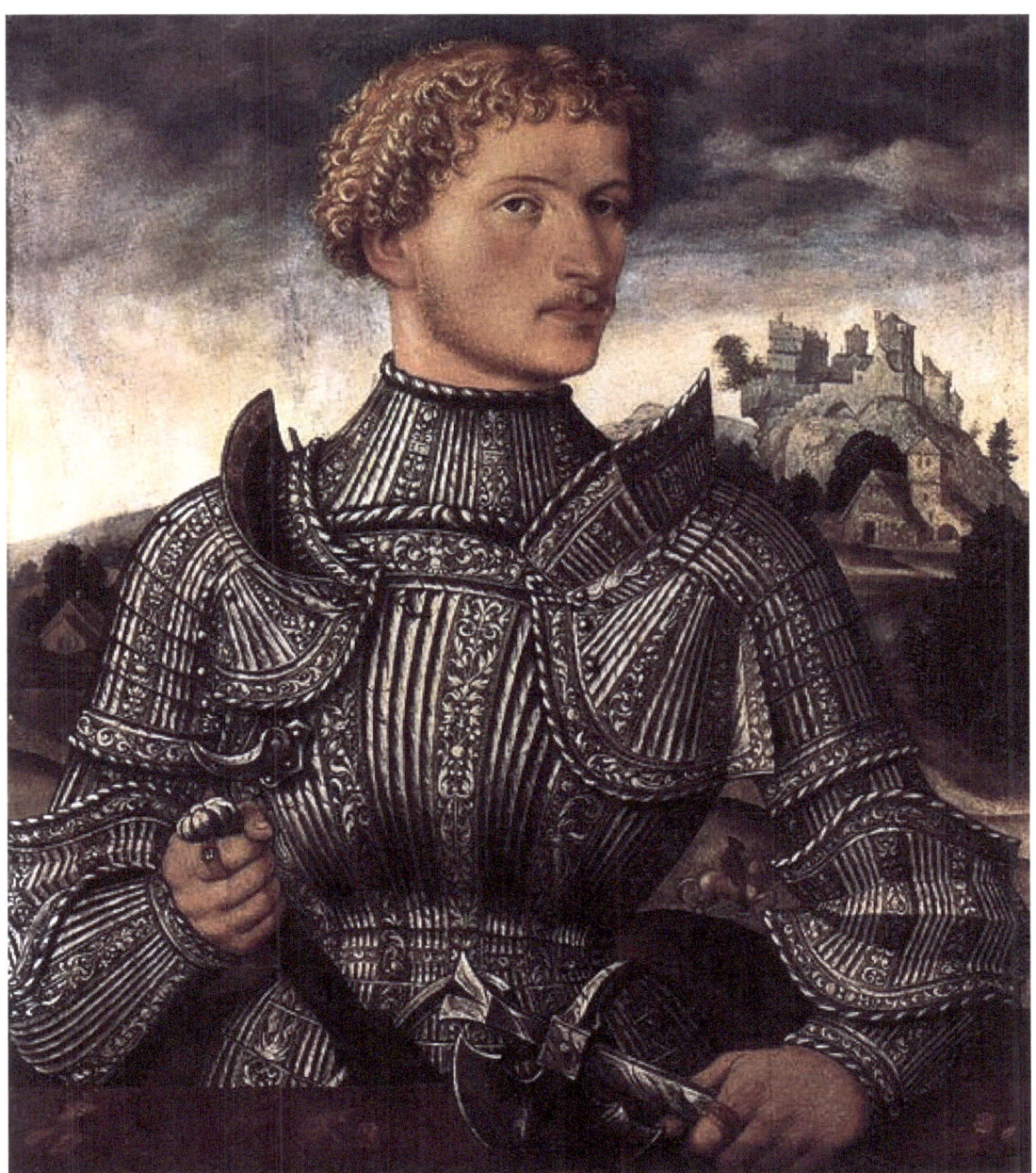

A Knight of the Rehlinger Family

Unknown artist. German Master, working in Ausburg around 1540

1540

Linden Wood

18.9in x 18.1 in

Gemäldegalerie, Berlin

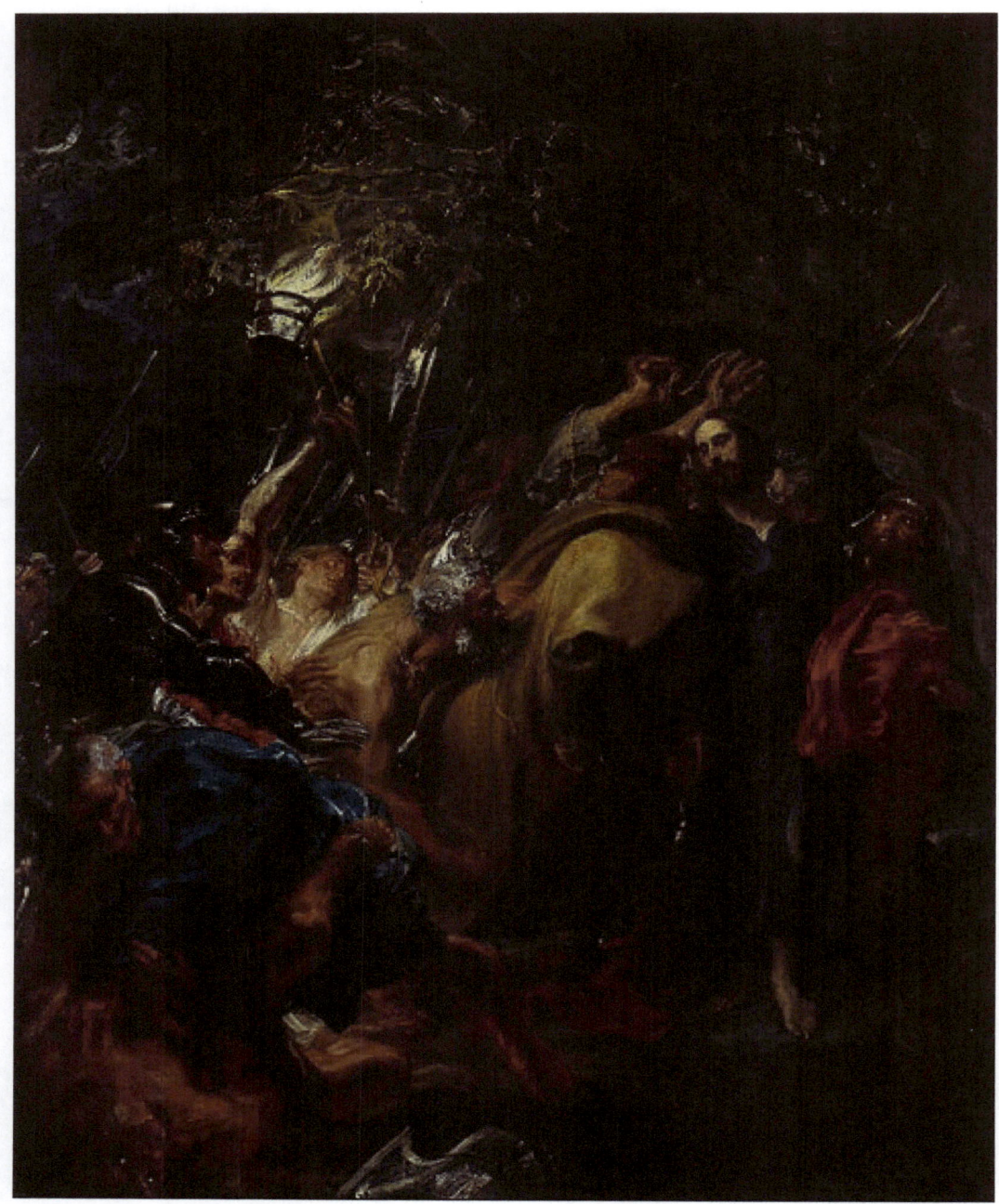

The Betrayal of Christ

Anthony Van Dyck

1608/1630

Oil on Canvas

44.5in x 55.88in

Minneapolis Institute of Art

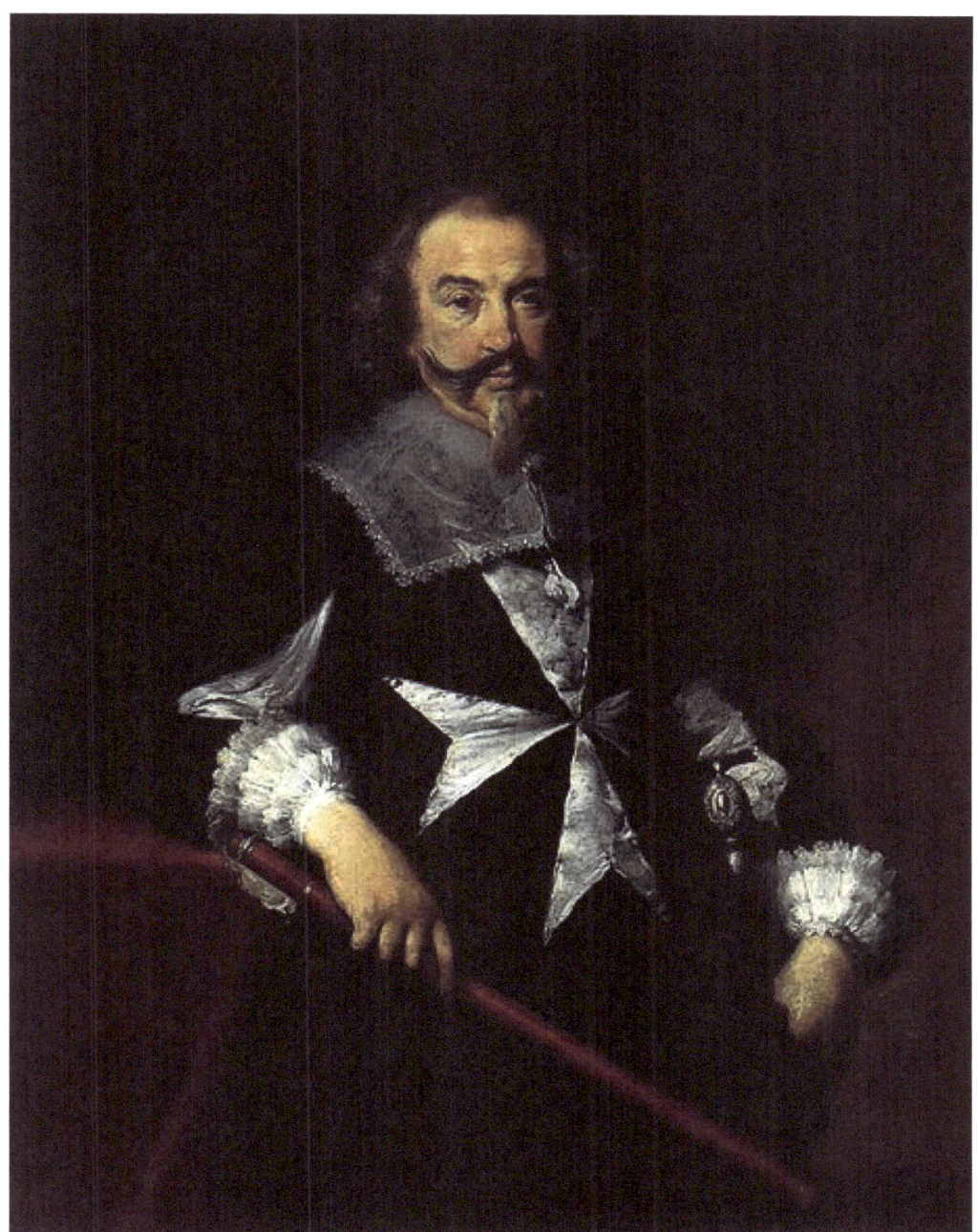

Portrait of a Maltese Knight

Bernardo Strozzi

Oil on Canvas

Painted in the first half of the 17th century

50.8in x 38.6in

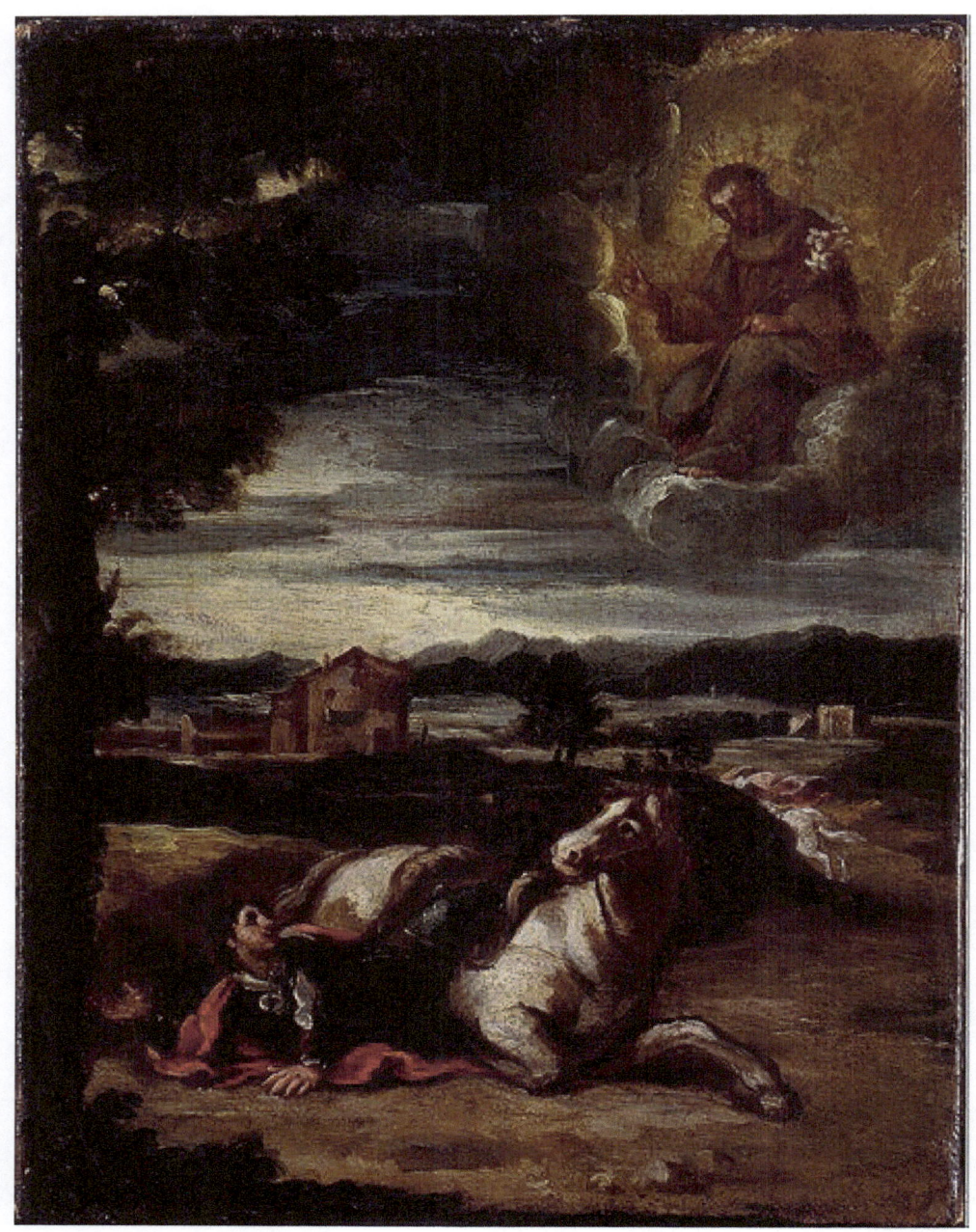

Saint Anthony of Padua appearing to a Knight

Spanish, author unknown/in dispute

17th century

Oil on Canvas

15.63in x 12.01in

Dulwich Picture Gallery

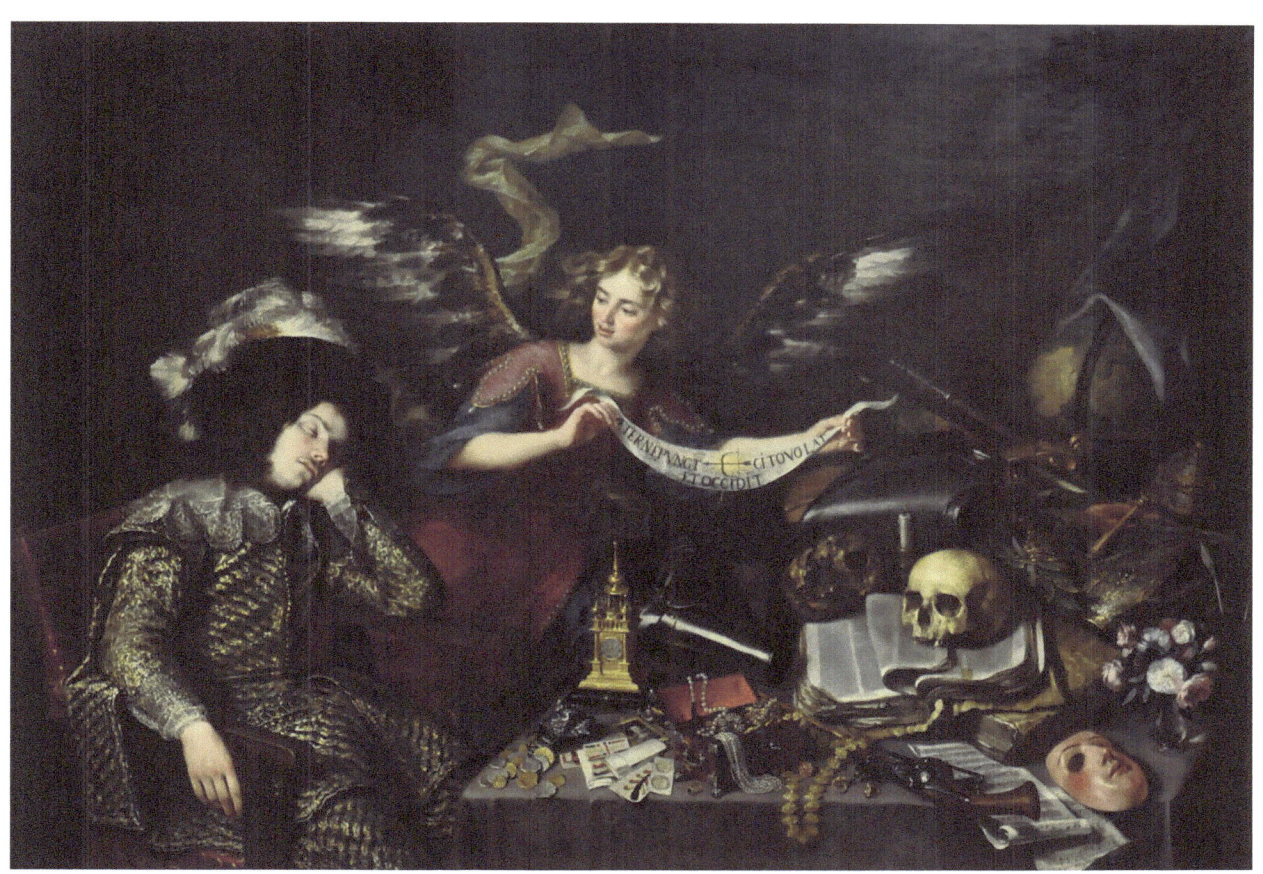

The Knight's Dream

Antonio de Pereda

1655

Oil on Canvas

85.4in x 59.8in

Royal Academy of Fine Arts of San Fernando

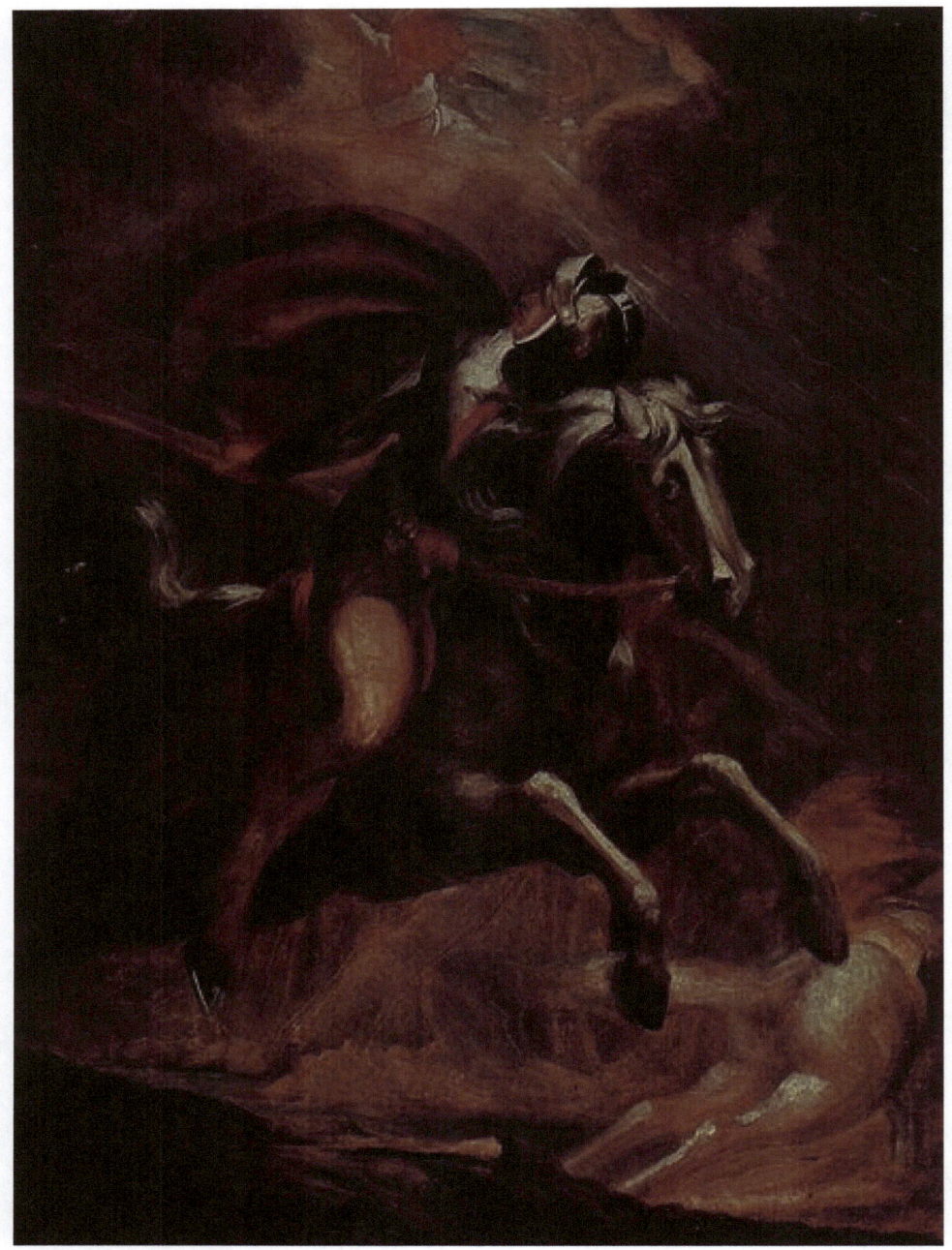

Cerasimus und Huon fliehen vor dem Elfenkönig Oberon

Henry Fuseli

1804-1805

Oil on Canvas

24in x 17.7in

Muraltengut

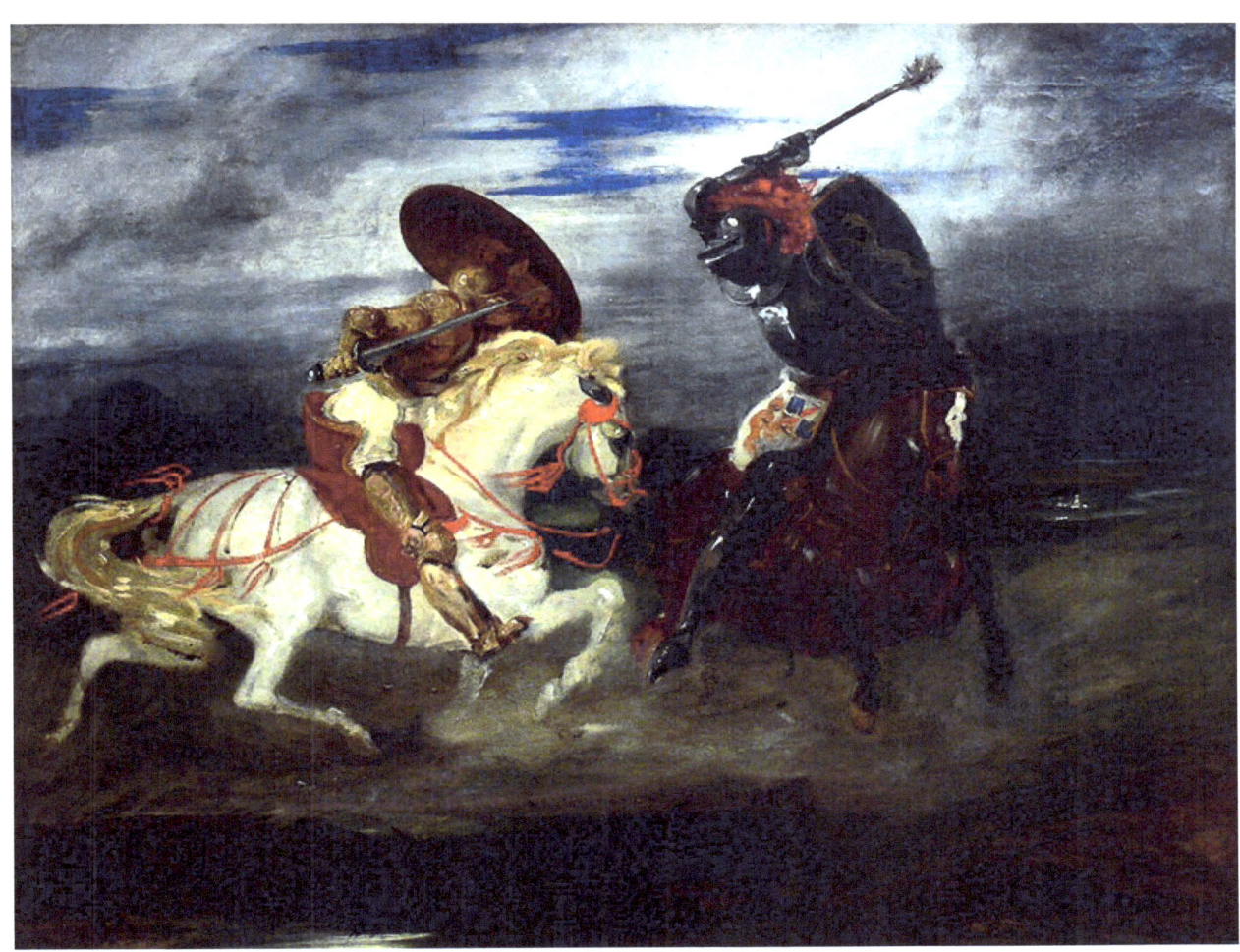

Combat de chevaliers dans la campagne

Eugene Delacroix

1824, estimated date

Oil on Canvas

31.9in x 41.3in

Louvre Museum, Paris

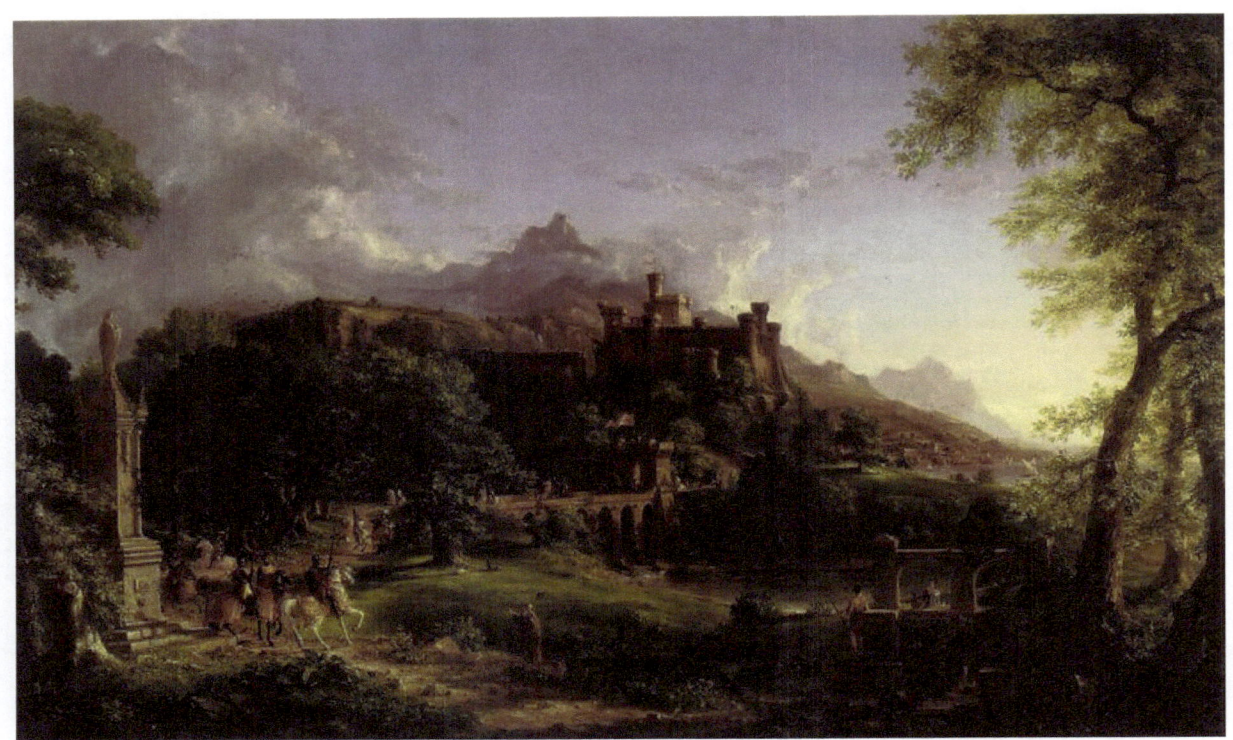

The Departure

Thomas Cole

1837

Oil on Canvas

39.5in x 63in

National Gallery of Art

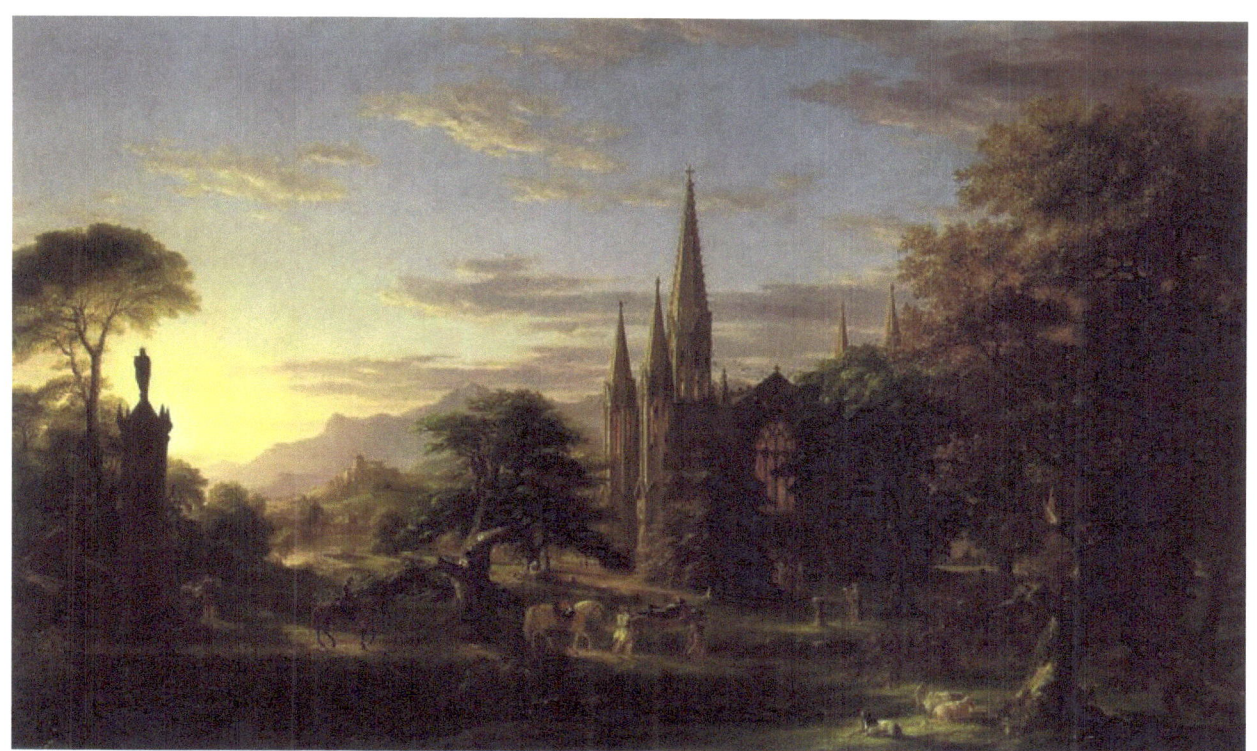

The Return

Thomas Cole

1837

Oil on Canvas

39.75in x 63in

Corcoran Gallery of Art

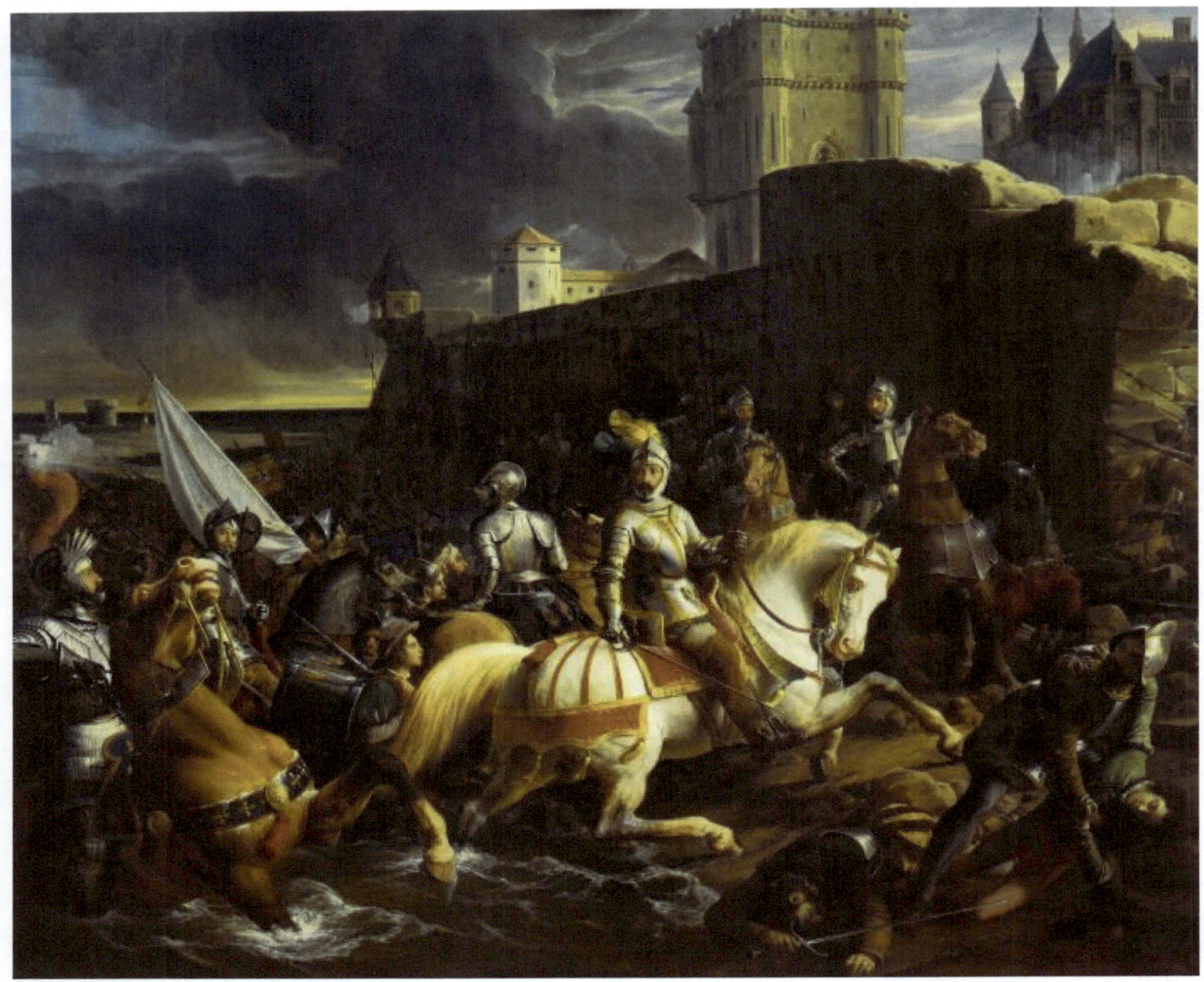

The Siege of Calais

Francois-Edouard Picot

1838

183.1in x 213.8in

Palace of Versailles

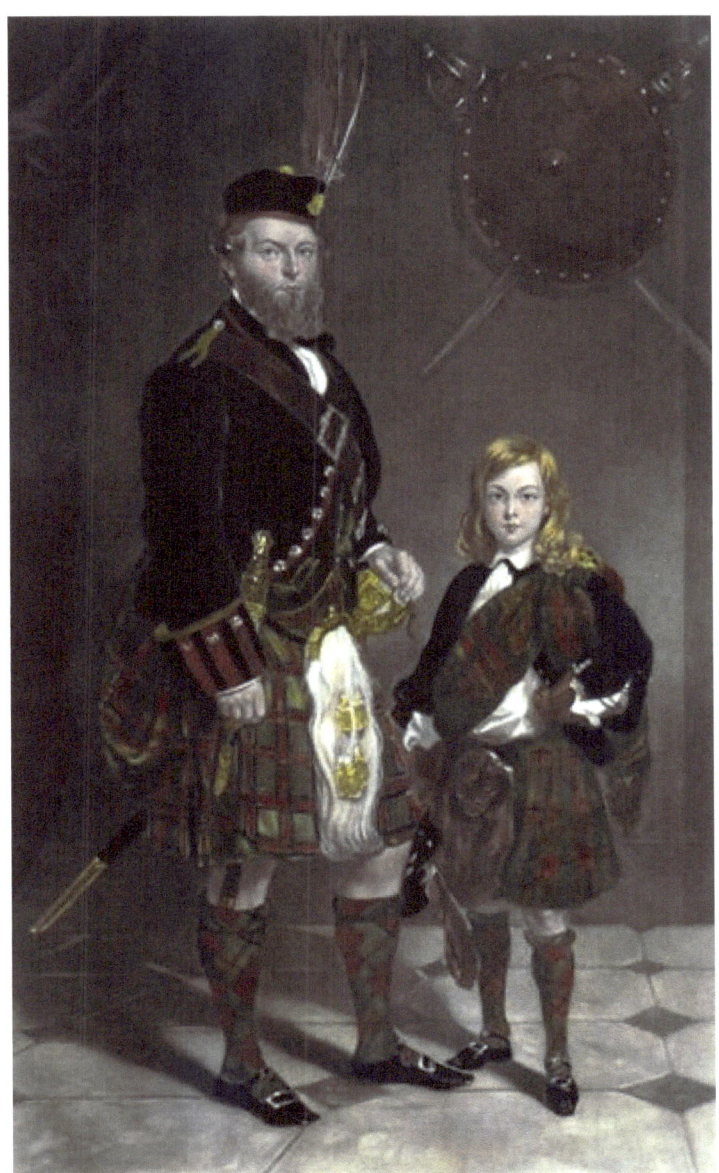

Knight of the Thistle

7th Earl of Seafield, John Ogilvy-Grant (1815-1881)

G. R. Ward

Engraving

from a picture by Sir Francis Grant

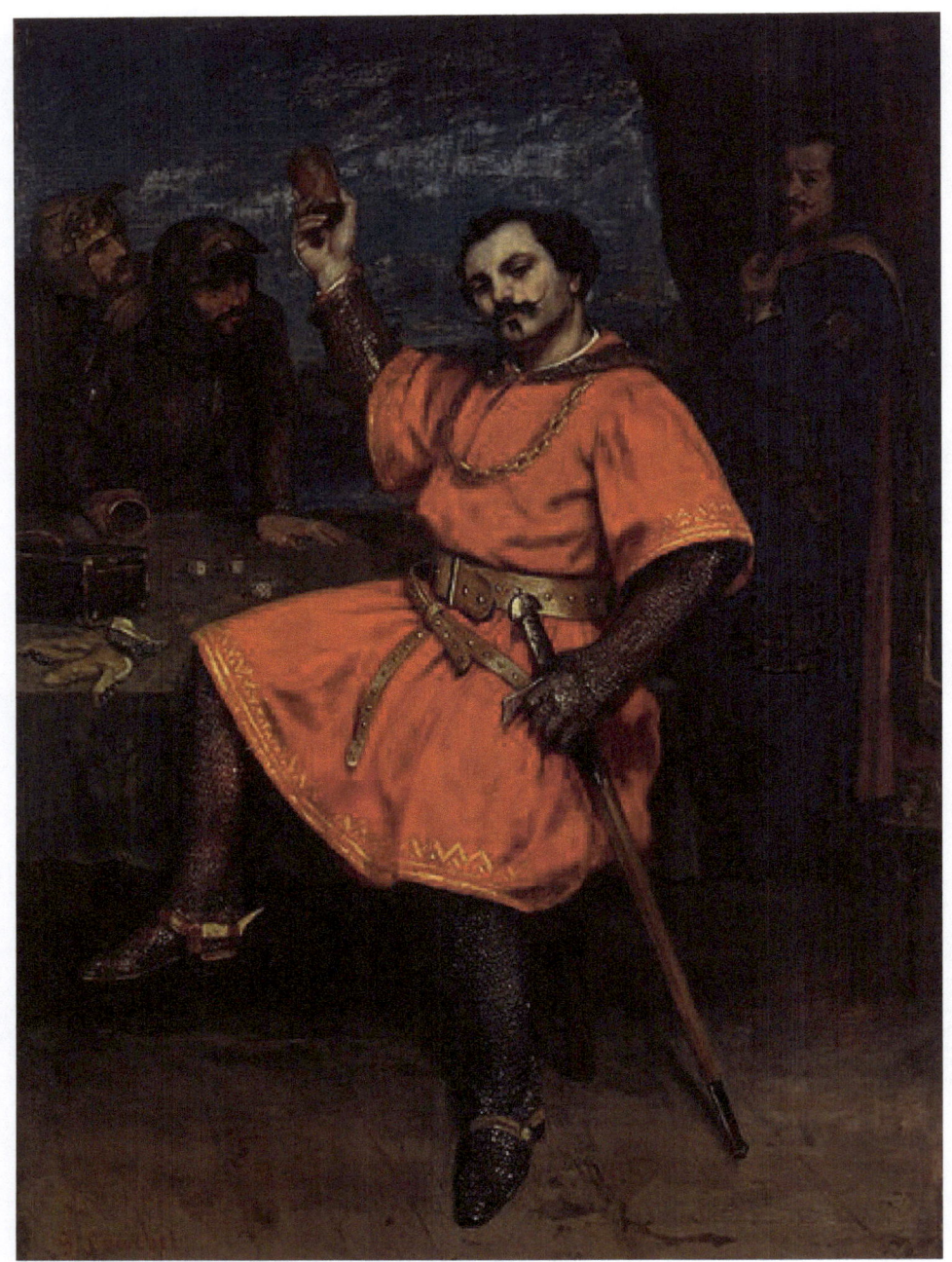

Portrait of Louis Gueymard as Robert le Diable

Gustave Corbet

1857

Oil on Canvas

58.5in x 42in

Metropolitan Museum of Art

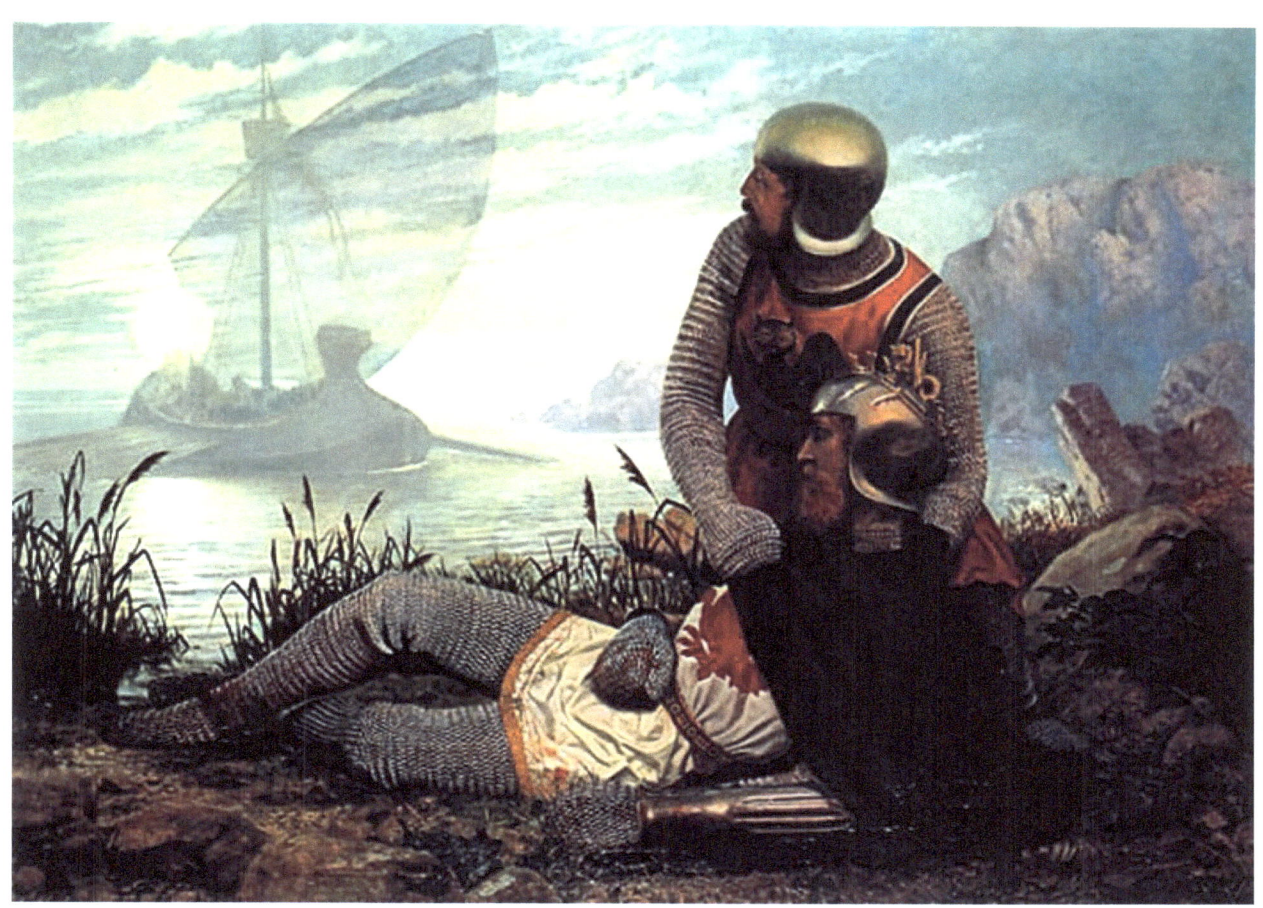

The Death of King Arthur

John Garrick

1862

Oil on Canvas

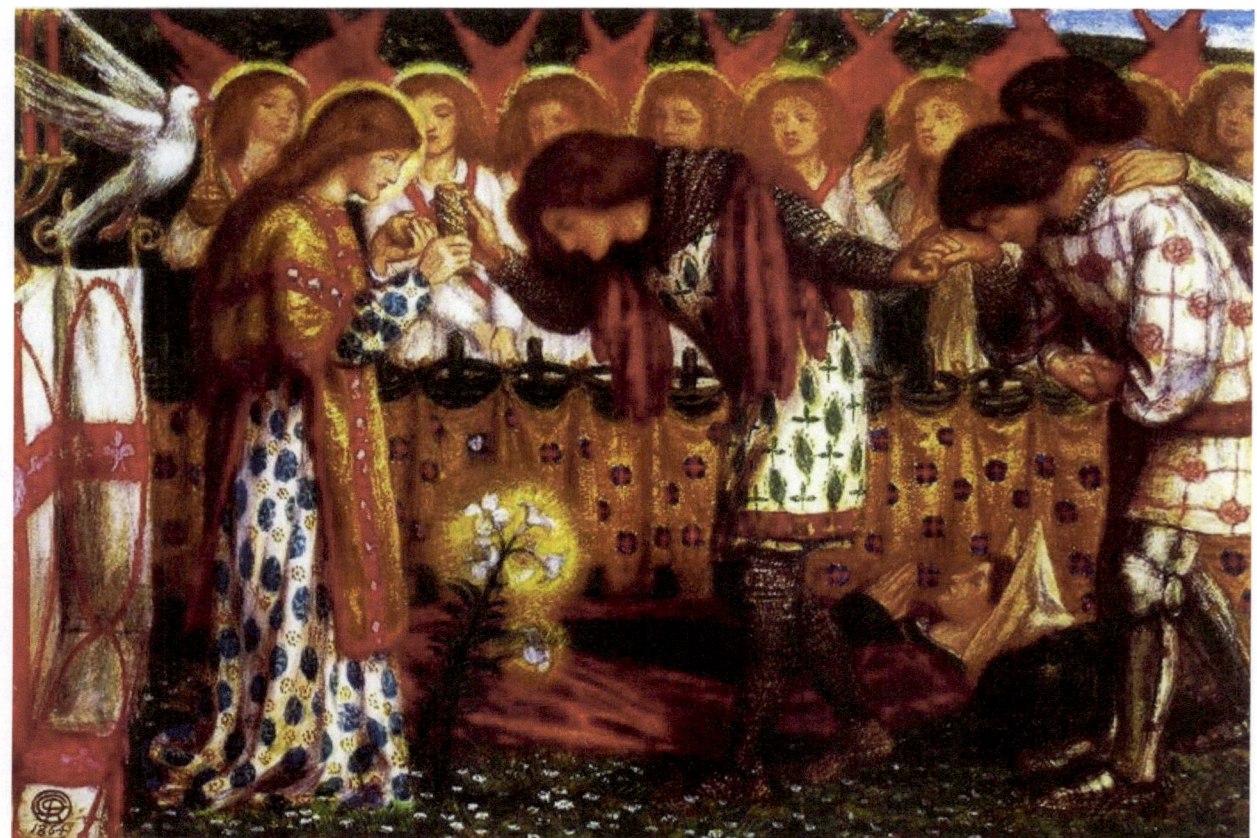

How Sir Galahad Sir Bors and Sir Percival were fed with the Sanc Grael; But Sir Percival's Sister Died by the Way

Dante Gabriel-Rossetti

1864

Watercolor

11.5in x 16.5in

Tate Britain, London, England

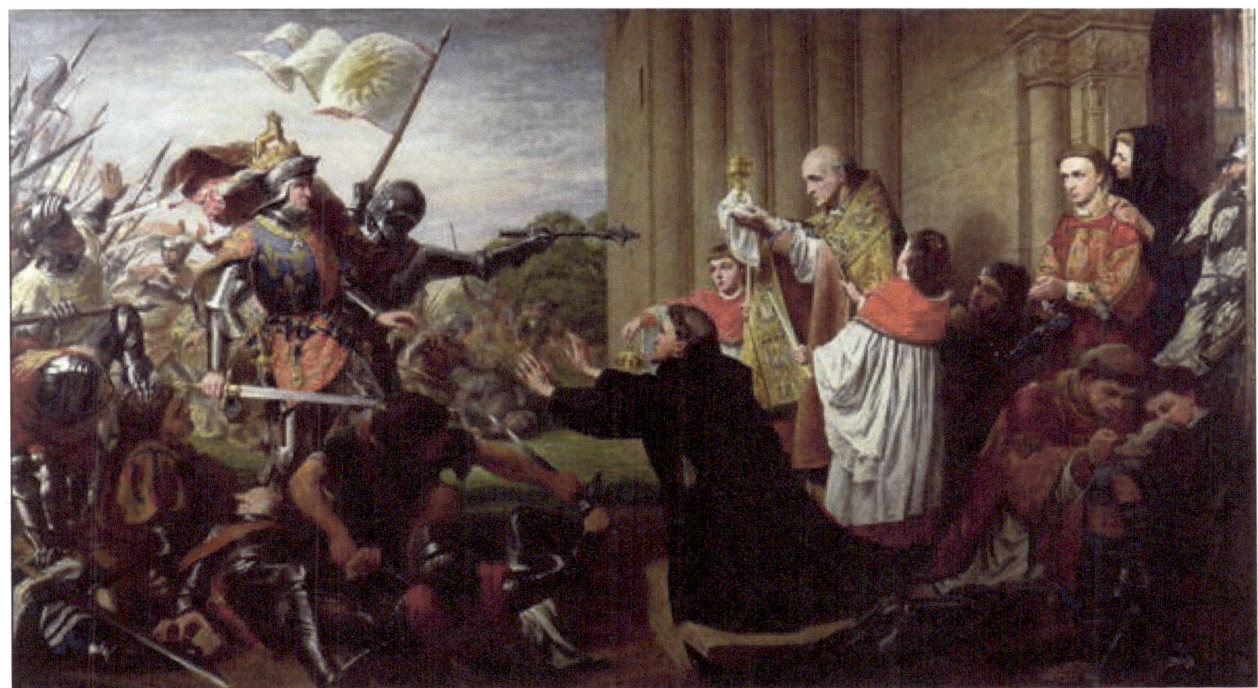

Sanctuary

— Edward IV and Lancastrian Fugitives at Tewkesbury Abbey
— aka Edward IV Withheld by Ecclesiastics from Pursuing Lancastrian Fugitives into a Church
Richard Burchett

1867

Oil on Canvas

61in x 108in

Guildhall Art Gallery & London's Roman Amphitheatre

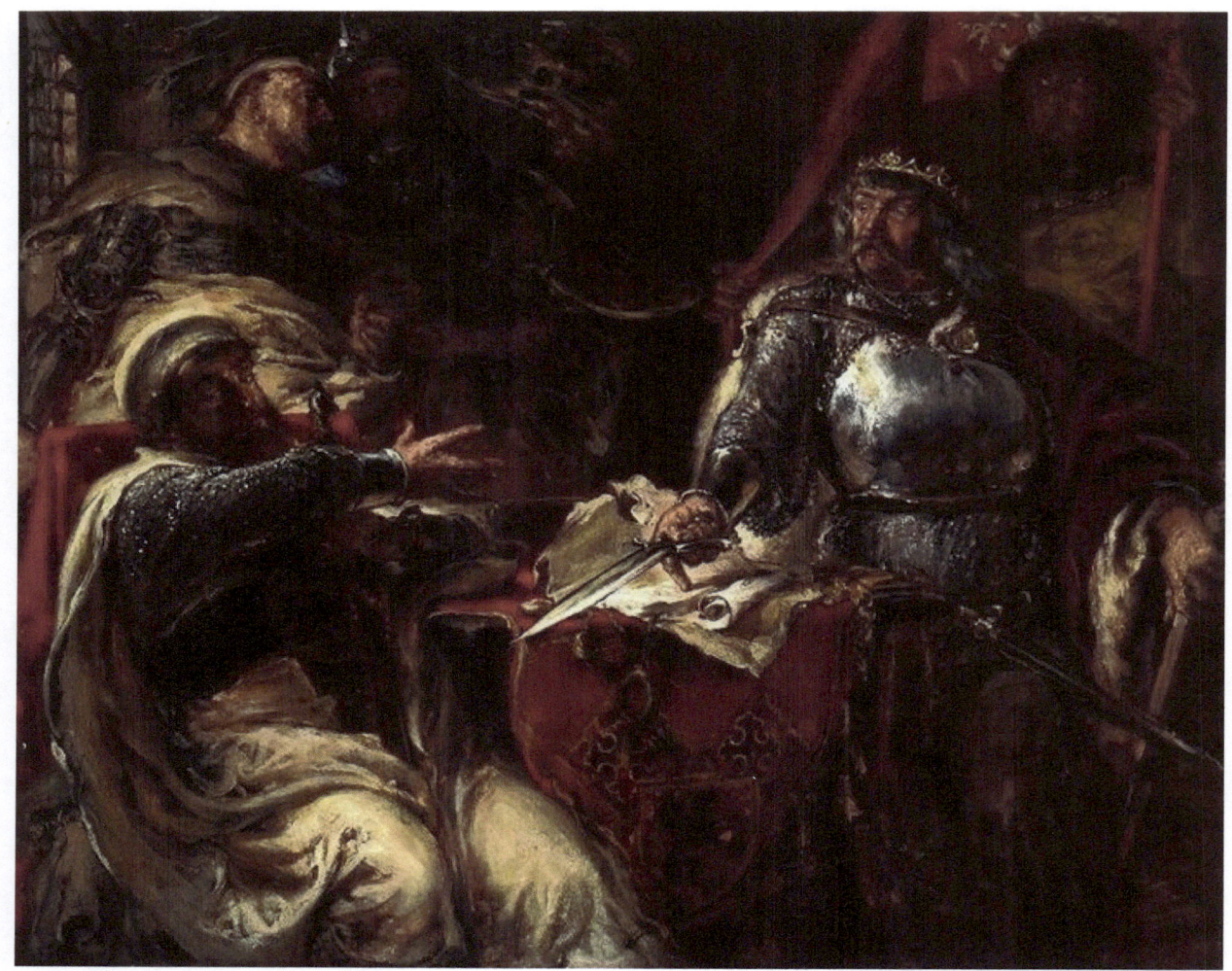

King Ladislaus the Elbow-high breaking off agreements with the Teutonic Knights at Brześć Kujawski.

Jan Matejko

1879

Oil on Oak

13.2in x 15.6in

National Museum in Warsaw

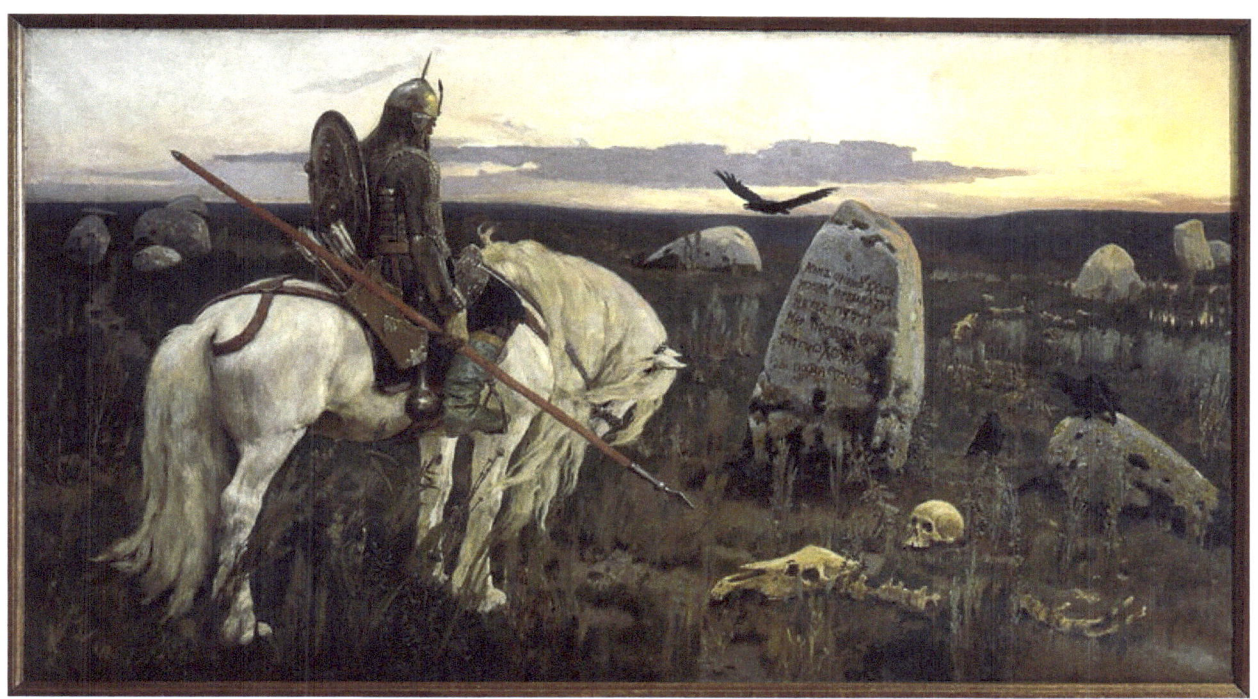

Knight at the Crossroads

Viktor M. Vasnetsov

1882

Oil on Canvas

State Russian Museum

The inscription on the rock is found in several Russian folk tales. To the effect of

"If you ride to the left, you will lose your horse. If you ride to the right, you will lose your head."

The horse and human skulls symbolize the words of the inscription.

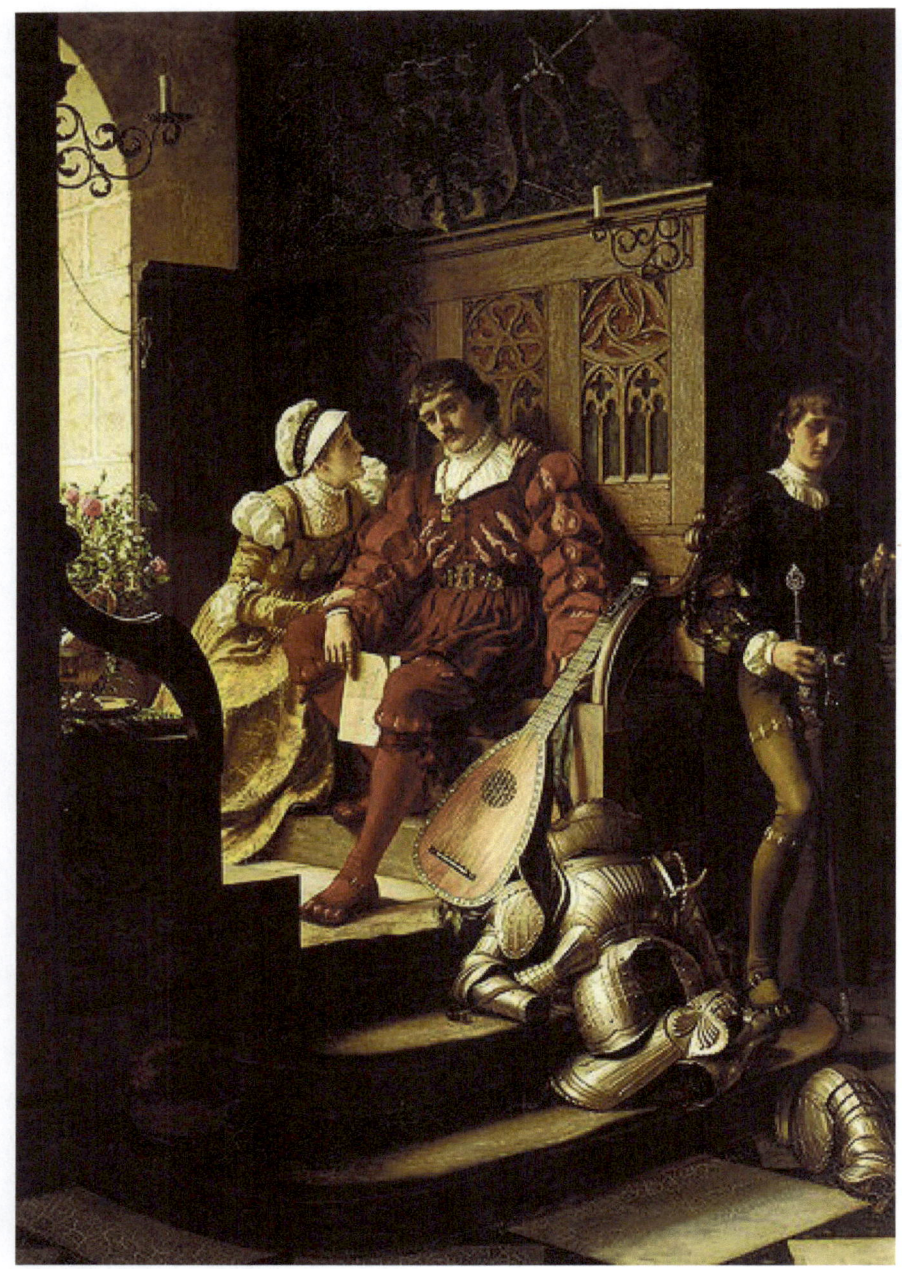

Duty

Edmund Blair Leighton

1883

Oil on Canvas

58in x 40.08in

Private Collection

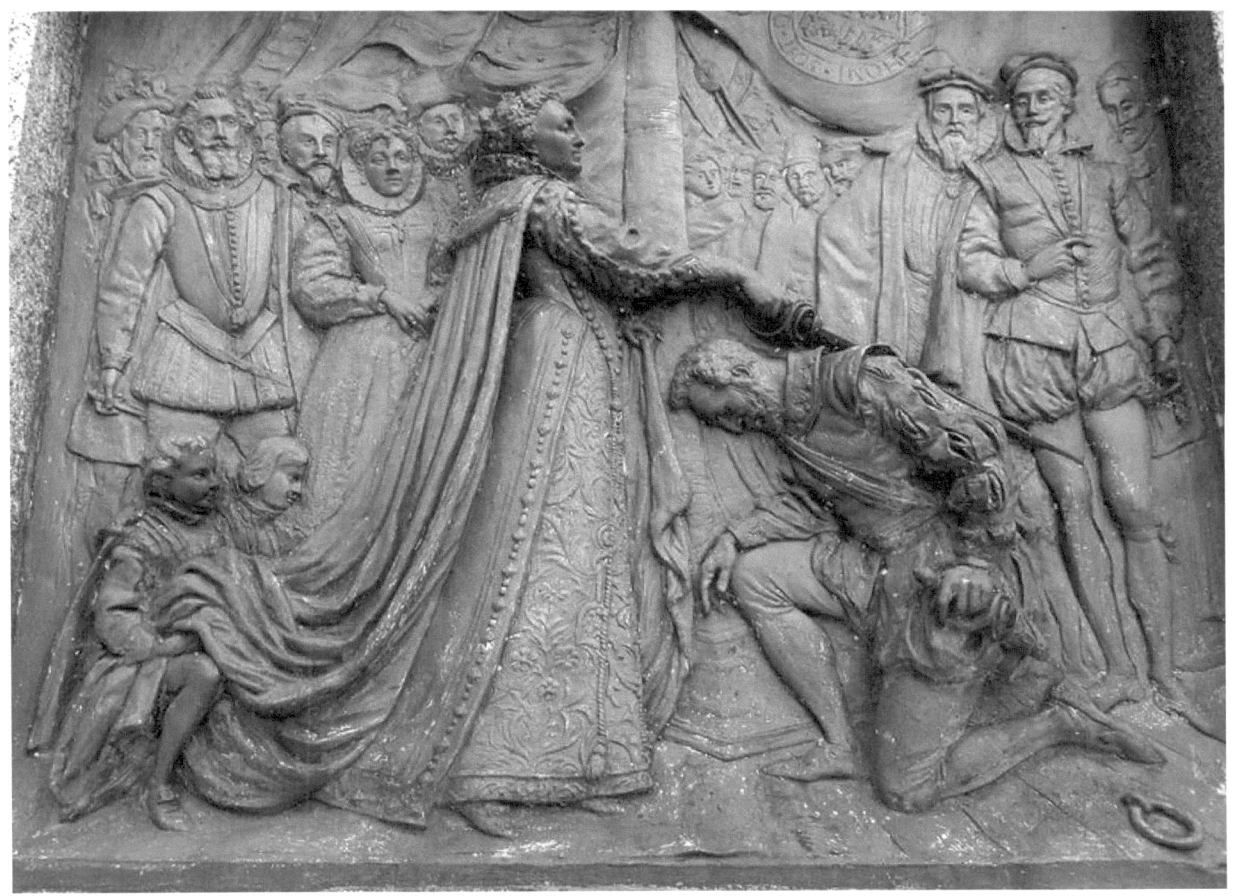

Sir Francis Drake knighted by Queen Elizabeth

Joseph Boehm

1884

One of 4 bronze relief plaques on the base of the Drake statue

Tavistock, Devon. The home town of Sir Francis Drake.

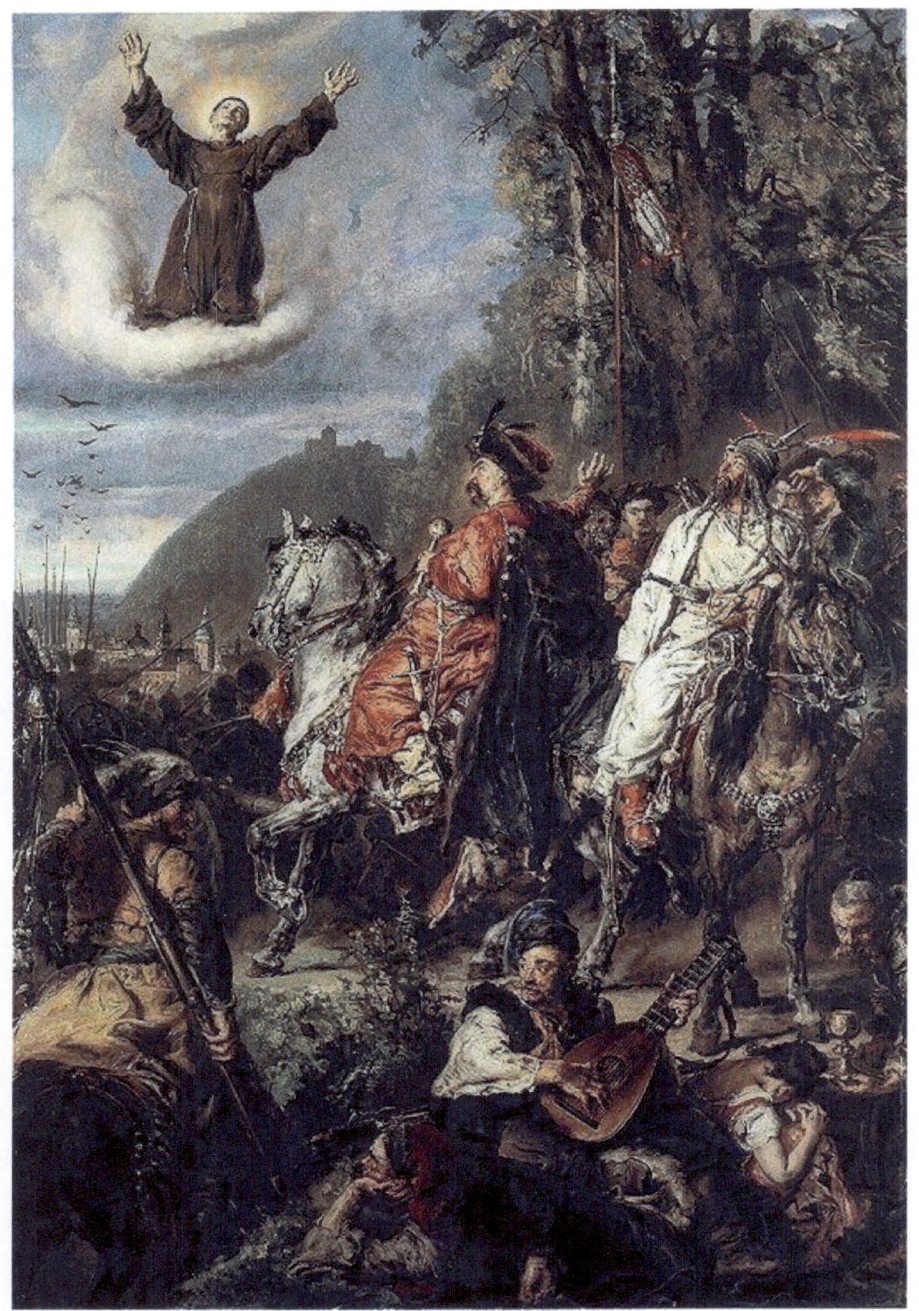

Bohdan Khmelnytsky with Tuhaj Bej near Lviv

Jan Matejko

1885

Oil on Panel

31.1in x 51.2in

National Museum in Warsaw

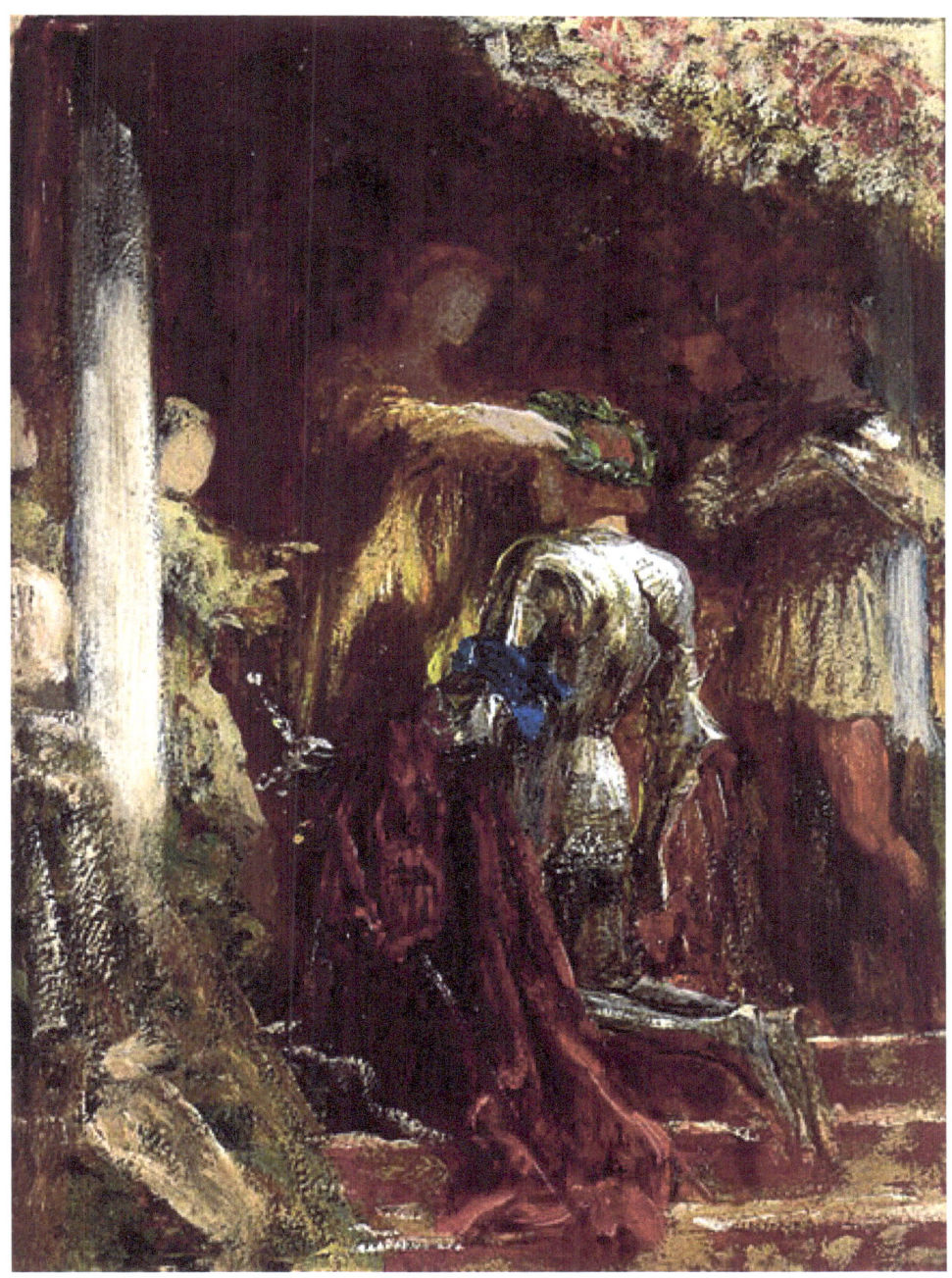

Victory, A Knight Being Crowned With A Laurel-Wreath

Frank Dicksee

After 1900

Oil on Board

11.2in x 8.2in

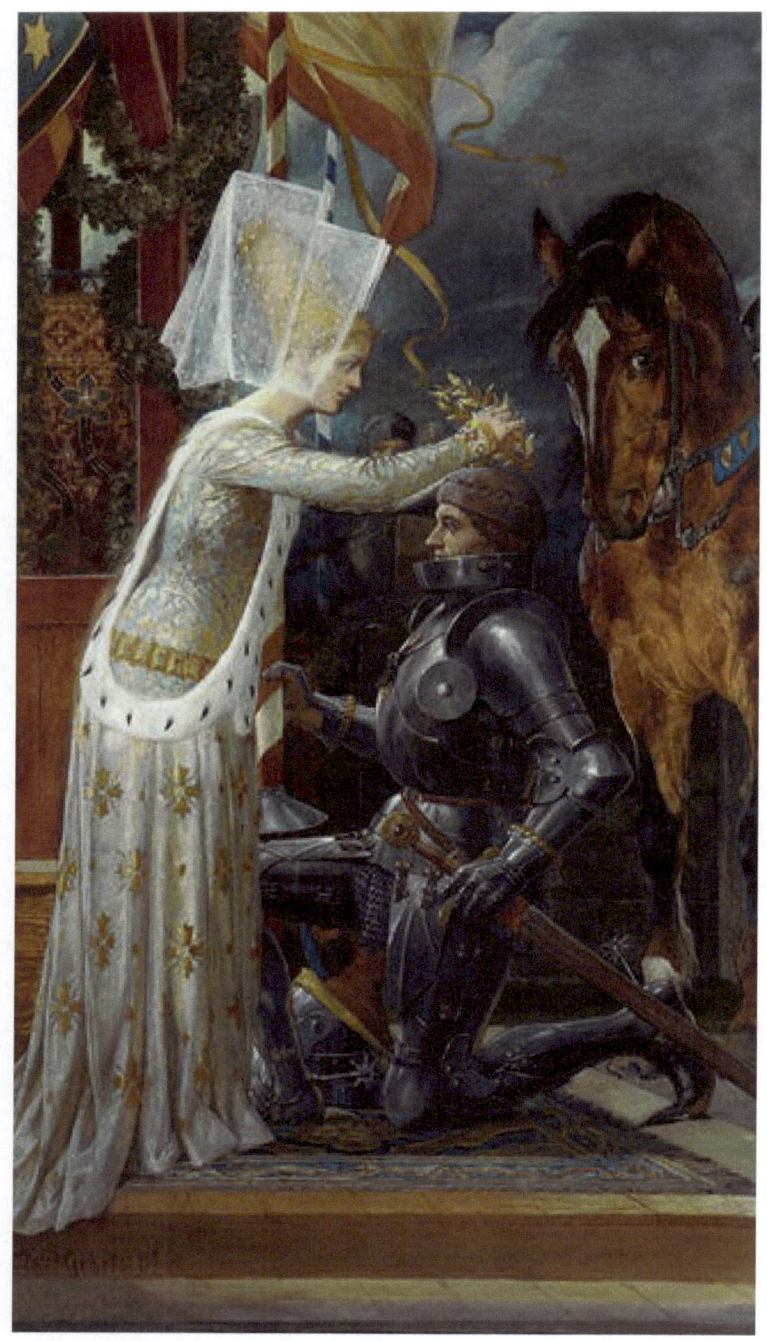

Ritter Ivanhoe

Johannes Gehrts

Between 1873 and 1921

Gouache

26.8in x 15in

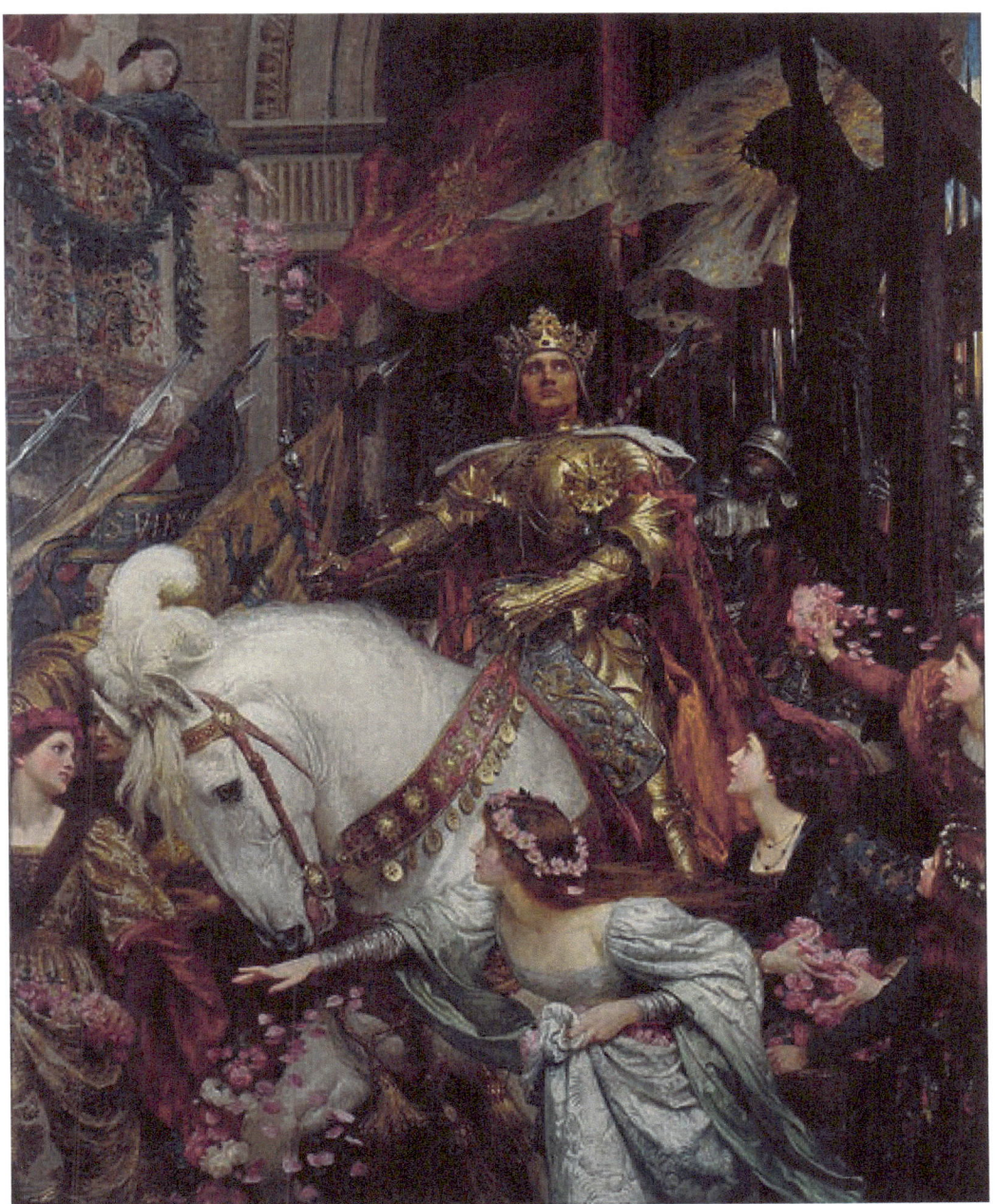

Two Crowns

Frank Dicksee

1900

Oil on Canvas

909.8in x 717.7in

Tate Britain

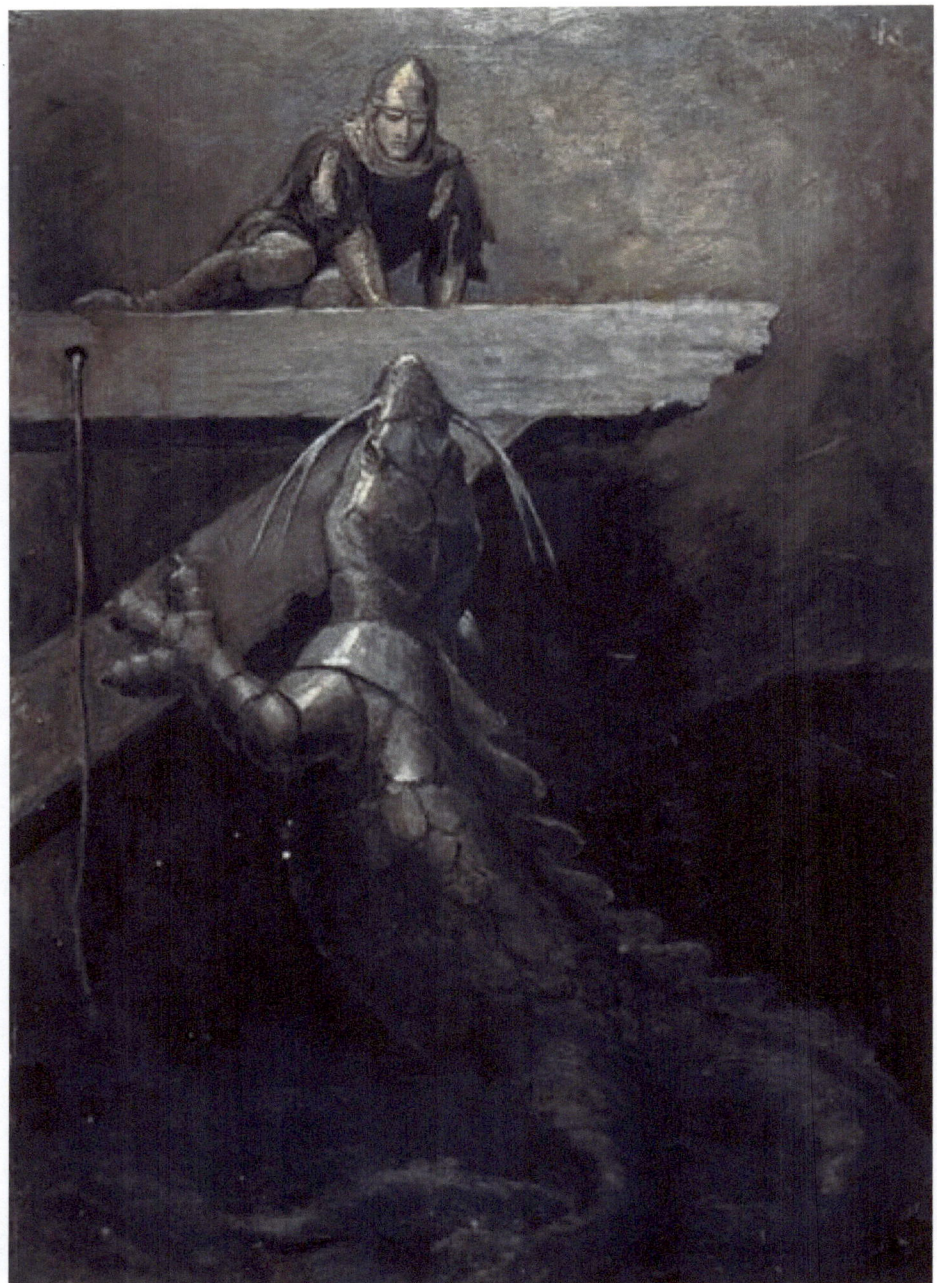

Dragon rearing up to reach medieval knight on ledge

Katherine Pyle

1932

Oil on Board

Published in *Charlemagne & His Knights* by Katharine Pyle, J.B. Lippincott Co., 1932

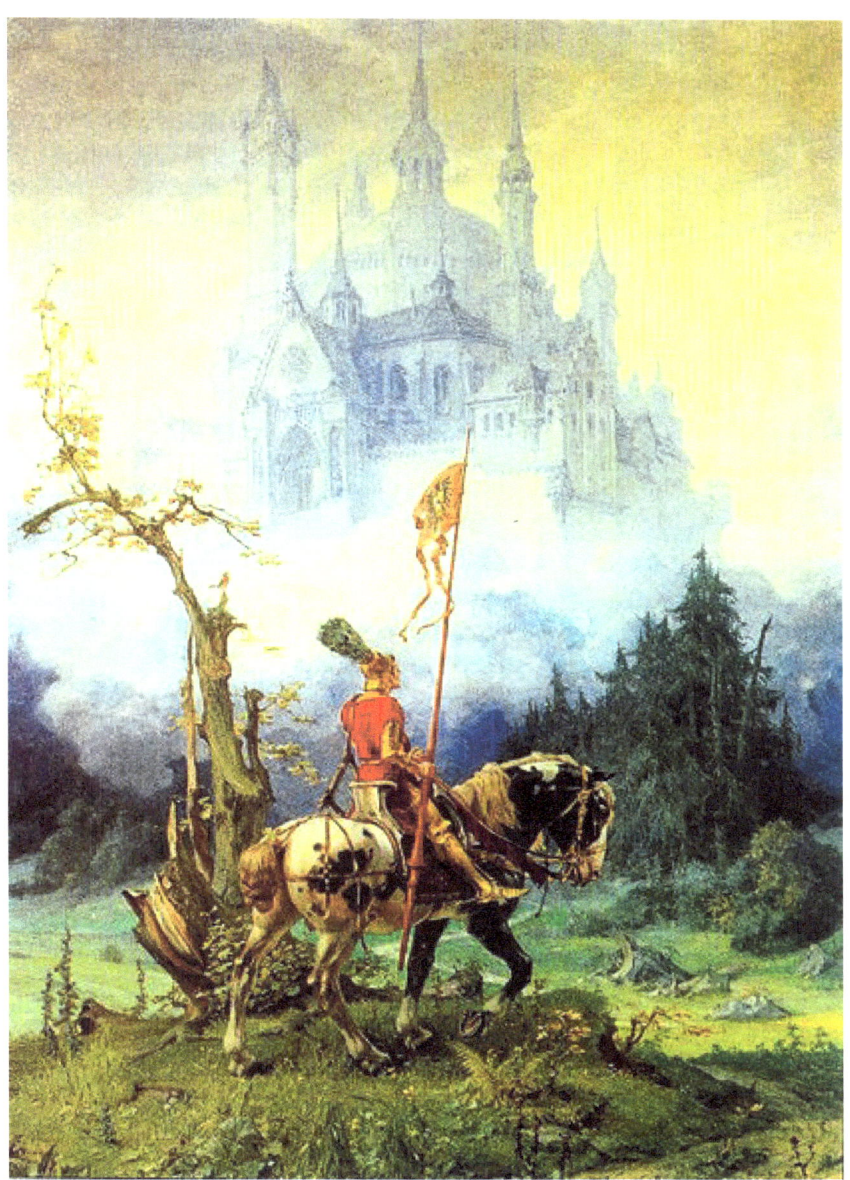

Percival

1934

Oil on Canvas

Martin Wingand